THE BUCKS VILLAGE BOY

by
Vic Hawes

Best wishes

Edited and Published by Vic Hawes
Copyright Reserved

ISBN 0 9524298 1 0

Printed by Parchment (Oxford) Limited, Printworks, Crescent Road,
Cowley, Oxford OX4 2PB

1994

CONTENTS

Acknowledgements

I wish to thank all who loaned me their treasured photographs, and so kindly helped me in dating and identifying the people on them. I thank you all.

Tom & Dorothy Baker	Rita Milne
Reg Harman	Joe Boyles
Bertha Neil & her sister Agnes	Linda Neil
Angie Folkes	Freda Hornett
Albert Hawes	Ada Dodwell
Albert Joiner	Joan Mott
Dolly Neil	

By the same author
"WORMINGHALL"
(Wornall in the 1920's)

Preface

Many autobiographies of country life appear to have been written by the sons or daughters of farmers, or at least by someone from the background of well to do families, someone "better off" as it were, in both standing and education. Whereas my upbringing was generated in one of the poorest sections of the rural community; that of the farm labourer.

In the recording of my childhood the aim is to give the younger reader a glimpse of what simple country life was like after the first World War and up to the early 1930's, at the same time to put the names of the ordinary people who lived at Worminghall, a small village in Buckinghamshire, into print so they shall not be forgotten, and in an inornate way give them a place in its modest history, and to show them the honour and respect I feel they deserve.

Worminghall, like most other villages of that time was more or less a self contained community, having its own Post Office, a small grocers' shop; public house; a carrier and his cart; blacksmith's shop; church; school and almshouses for the elderly. There were other visiting services such as fruiterer and eggler, several butcher's carts, the local policeman and district nurse both astride their bicycles. The nurse called at the school regularly. The policeman occasionally, mainly to let the potential wrong doer be aware of the law, and to instil a little bit of fear into his or her mind. Besides all this there was a midwife who could be called upon at any time, night or day, as too there was a special lady to wash and lay out the dead. The sexton was also the official grave digger. There was an undertaker-cum-coffin maker in the next village, a mile away at Ickford.

The only so called essential services Worminghall was short of was a bank, and those of a doctor and a solicitor – all available at the small market town of Thame – five miles away. While a bank was only needed by the very few such as farmers, the rest of the community could hardly afford doctors fees and only called upon him as a last, almost dying resort. Solicitors and their legal fees were only affordable by the "better off". Fortunately the vicar regularly visited the whole of his parishioners, and being an educated man would advise and comfort them according to their needs, to the best of his ability and his purse would allow; make sure the very poor were fed and clothed; ever supported and assisted by his good lady wife, and other ladies of the parish.

Although, in general life was hard, and to many, existence a struggle, they seemed quite content with their lot, and never complained. They respected their marriage vows, and other people's property, disciplined their children, and brought them up in a Christian community with the Church as its centre. Drugs were taboo. Of course, there were pranks by the young, but no vandalism and graffiti, muggings, child molestations and sexual assaults were unheard of; the longer I live the more I realise the people of my era had the joy of knowing "Old England" at her very best. With these self same people undoubtedly being the main contributing factor to that excellence'. At the same time becoming aware that my childhood days were among the happiest of my life.

V.H.

Chapter I
The Common

The world of the young is very small, my little world was shared with Mum and Dad who were my foster parents together with mother, my real mother, our Jack, Harold and Kath.

Later, when I asked about my real father, I was told he had been in the secret service, was sent on a mission abroad and never returned-missing-assumed lost while on active service. Not that I was very concerned anyway; I all ready had a dad, and luckier than most – two mums. I suppose Jack and Harold were termed as my foster brothers and Kath as my foster sister. However, being so young the relationship was of little account, the only relationship I knew in those early days was, they were all part of my life with 'Mum' being the key figure. Our home was two thatched cottages joined into one with two flights of stairs being its main feature. Situated in the middle of the fields and miles from anywhere which was known as the 'Common', and very isolated. The nearest village was a good two miles across the fields and down the lane to where Kath my sister attended school. Of course, this was completely out of my territory, which, in itself was confined to a radius of about one hundred yards, embracing the garden, the orchard, a very small paddock and a section of a spinney that housed the swing, its rope being attached to the convenient branch of an oak.

There were two ponds, one in the paddock, the other in the orchard (apart from the rainwater caught from the gutter of a small leanto hovel at the end of the house) were our only source of water. The one in the orchard providing our drinking water was fairly deep; Mum used to frighten me from going near it by saying. "If you get too near to that pond the old man will pull you in".

"Will I be able to get out?" I would ask. "No. He'll pull you right under, and I won't ever see you again. Just you keep away from those ponds my boy."

Her strategy certainly worked for I never got near enough to fall in. Though she slipped in once when scooping a bucket of water, she was very, wet, and succeeded in convincing me the 'old man' had pulled her in, but being strong she was able to get away and scramble out of his reach. I believed it, and was so happy she had escaped and I was able to sit on her lap, feeling all warm inside, and so very very safe; how I hated and feared that 'old man'.

I suppose the year would have been 1918 as I was born in 1915 its hardly likely my memory goes back to 1917. We left the common during the late summer of 1919 so my recollections of it would be during that period. Being out in the wilds, with the fields surrounding us, and being quite marshy it is not surprising there were quite a lot of snakes in the vicinity. One day I discovered a silvery one curled up asleep by the wall of the house. Dad always reckoned to kill snakes, so I ran indoors to Mum and told of my discovery, insisting she come and see it.

"Will you kill it Mum"? I asked.

"No. I'll cover it up with a pan, I expect Dad will kill it when he comes home". She said.

The pan referred to was a red earthenware panchion that served many domestic purposes. I have often wondered about their reason for the war on snakes, was it because they thought them dangerous, not knowing grass ones were innocuos, or was it just a thorough dislike of them as

The Old Home – Waterperry Common

they were often found indoors in the most unlikely places, giving who found them quite a turn. What ever the reason, I knew this one was doomed and so kept watch for Dad to come across the fields from the stable where he kept his piebald nag. After what seemed an eternity I saw him heading toward home, and ran to meet him. He took my hand in his big rough one, and before he could say anything. I said. "Dad, Mum has got a snake under the pan, she says you will kill it. Will you?"

"We'll see" He replied, not committing himself, not a bit excited. I was; when we reached the gate I had left open he said.

"Pop indoors and fetch my knobbed stick" I was off like a flash, probably falling over I was always falling over being in such a hurry I suppose, but more likely because I, like all little boys of my age was dressed in petticoats. "Mum, Dad's home". I shouted, adding. "He wants his stick".

"You know where it is". She said.

Yes there it was in its place behind the outside door; Dad always kept it there in case of robbers, he had a gun too – Dad was very brave and not afraid of anything. I always felt safe when he was around. Grabbing the stick I managed to give myself a clout with it. "Come on Mum," I shouted, as I dashed out of the door, dragging the stick behind me. The moment I had been waiting for was near. Mum followed me out. Dad took hold of the stick at its end, and held it up in a striking position.

"Right. You pick up the pan Jane". Dad often called mum Jane. I was not allowed to. "Stand back boy". He ordered. I promptly stepped back a couple steps, tripped over the cat, and sat on my backside. At this moment Mum picked up the pan, and there it was – gone. I could not believe my eyes, there was no snake to be seen. Dad laughed. "You sure there was a snake there".

"Of course there was". Snapped Mum. "Mmm! Dad lifted up his cap. Scratched his bald head, and exclaimed. "I reckon the pan wasn't quite flat all the way round. Daresay 'twas lodged up on a bit of stick, and it managed to slither out".

"I don't know about that". Retorted Mum, then added with a smile.

"I expect the cat had it".

Whenever anything went missing in our house, and could not be found, the cat always got the blame. Sometimes Dad would add. "Ah! A two legged one I shouldn't wonder". I never did see that two legged cat. It was some years before the 'penny dropped". At this point Mum went indoors.

"Come and have your tea". She called. Dad and I did not need a second bidding, and anyway, unless we hurried the cat might have it.

Both of my big brothers were in the army. 'Our Jack' was home on convalescence. He had been wounded, and had the evidence to prove it in the shape of a lead ball, the size of a small marble which had been removed from his head, kept wrapped in cotton-wool, and proudly shown to all and sundry throughout the years to follow.

At the time of my recollection poor Jack was very poorly. I was constantly being told to keep quiet with such remarks as – "Just you keep quiet young man. Jack's head is bad. I shan't tell you again". Not that I intended making a noise, I used to forget.

As Jack grew stronger we took him for walks in the orchard; he held Mum's arm on one side whilst I held her hand on the other – playing quite a part in the exercising of our hero. Possibly Mum thought it better to take me along so she knew what I was up to. After a while, when he could go out on his own, he had to 'go back'.

Just what 'going back' entailed I knew not, but it was not long before Jack was out of the army, and back in what was called Civvy Street.

Harold came home on leave, and announced this was his last before going out to the Far East, which I later learned was Hong Kong, and that he transferred from the army into prison service, as a warder.

He never came home again though he used to write to Mum from time to time until, eventually his letters dried up completely.

I had no affection for Harold. In fact, that last time he came home I grew to positively dislike him.

Mum used to make a special kind of home made physic which she

"Our Jack"
Jack Brown alias Atkins on the left, with his pal Jack Lively. They both suffered head wounds during the great war.

4

gave to the family, and to me whenever I had a sniffle. 'In case it developed into a cold' she said: How I detested that physic. Harold knew this, and undoubtedly delighted in teasing me by pretending to dose me with it. Taking hold of the bottle in one hand, and a spoon in the other he would say. "Hold him Mum". Mum's response was to put her arm round me, and tell him to. 'Pack it in'. Laughing he would dodge round one side of her and then the other to try and grab me, not happy until he had succeeded in making me cry. A success never long delayed.

He knew he was only teasing, and so did Mum, but this was not so with a three year old. I have never really understood how teasing seems to give to a certain type of person such pleasure. Possibly that early experience resulted in my growing up with the general conception that, to tease a small child, or torment a weaker character than oneself is about the lowest form of treatment one person can inflict upon another. Regarding the latter, whenever it has been in my power to do so, I have intervened, sometimes physically, to defend victims from such dispicable behaviour.

In later years, when I asked Mum to lend me some money for one of my hair'brained schemes. She told me, she once saved twenty pounds. Lent it to Harold the last time he came home on leave, but had not seen him or any of the money since, so had never again saved money. This news served to confirm my established opinion of Harold. He was nothing more than a rotter and a cad, and his absence from our lives no loss. Though I am sure Mum would not have agreed, that being the way mums are.

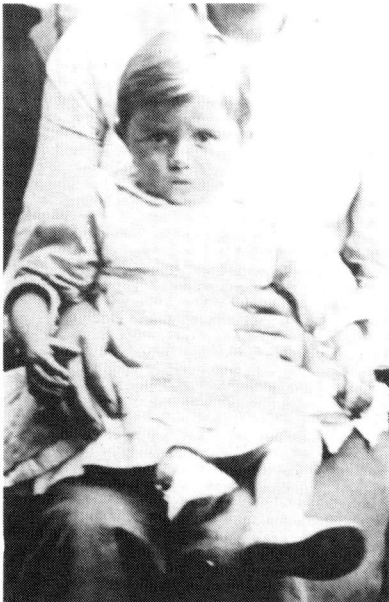

Me as a little-un   5

Chapter II

High Jinks

Our Kath was about ten years older than me; when Mum was busy and Kath was home, it became her lot to look after me.

Sometimes on a Saturday Mum would catch the carrier's cart at Waterperry Towns'end, and go off to Oxford, leaving us on our own for most of the day. Then we would have high jinks; all sorts of games. She would start off giving me a swing; then, when we tired of that play houses, making mud pies, using tinlids, and old saucers for utensils, with bricks for a fireplace.

Kath was quite an expert in culinary practices, in fact, in later life she graduated from kitchen maid to cook. No wonder the making of her concoctions kept me busy fetching this and that, often being told. 'Don't touch that'or. 'Leave that alone'. An order often accompanied by a little slap. She never hurt me, just wanted to assert her authority, after all she was in charge during Mum's absence, so I accepted her punishment with little protest, not often I kicked her puddings over, or stuck my fingers in her cakes.

She always referred to our accomplishments as 'hers'. This was no doubt that predominant self coming to the fore together with that individuality to which most little girls are accustomed. Kath could be described as being fairly bossy, though it was not often I told on her, and when I did was greeted with the chanting of.

> "Tell tell tit,
> Your tongue shall be slit,
> And all the the little puppy dogs,
> Shall have a little bit".

This showed up at that early stage in life, tale telling was a contemptable thing, and in my case, proved to be a lasting cure.

One of our shared secrets, and we had many, was a pastime enacted when Mum was away. Kath would invariably know how long she would be gone; as soon as Mum was across the pasture and out of sight she would get Dad's bike out of the hovel, and give me rides around the orchard. She would sit me on a cushion on the crossbar. I seemed miles up in the air, and hung tightly to the handlebars; then she would hold the handle grips, this meant her arms were bent round me lending a bit more support and at the same time adding to what little confidence I already had.

With much laughter and excite'ment she would manoeuvre the pedal to the desired position, put her leg under and through the crossbar, and push off, wobbling all over the place as she pedalled, hitting the humps and bumps; often we would come a cropper, but it never seemed to hurt or deter us except one day, Kath got a bit too near the ditch, and pitched me into the stinging nettles.

Needless to say, I bawled my head off, bringing our fun and games to an abrupt conclusion. Kath did her best to comfort me; she collected some dock leaves, spat on them and applied them to the affected parts. Although this failed to cure the tingling it was very cooling, causing me to wet myself, the combination being to some extent pacifying. It stopped me bawling.

I think that was the day I had my first lesson in the deviation from truth. Kath instructed me on what to say, or rather, not to say, but 'just leave everything to her'. She would tell Mum we went for a walk down the orchard, that I got too near to the ditch and fell in.

Supposedly Mum was not particularly worried so long as there was nothing seriously amiss. Seeing that I was always falling over Kath's story was quite convincing. Addressing me, Mum said.

Kath in the role of nursemaid

7

"Never mind it'll be better in the morning".

Mum always said that, and as far as I remember she was invariably right.

Like all good things, our little escapade came to an end.

One day Mum had gone to the village. We had got the bike out as usual; whether Mum got a lift, or being so engrossed Kath lost all sense of time, I am not sure, but there she was, stood by the stile just as we got level with it.

"And what sort of a caper do you call this"? She asked.

"We were only having a little ride". Kath replied." As she got off and let the bike to the ground. Get that bike back where it belongs – Goodness knows what your dad will say, if he finds out".

From then on that little word *if* acquired a new meaning of no small significance. Kath was on to it like a shot. "Mum". She said. "You said *if* he finds out. You won't tell him, will you"?

The will you being as much statement as question.

"We'll see." Replied Mum. "It just depends how you behave during the next few days".

We'll be ever so good, honest we will". Said Kath. To which no doubt I nodded agreement.

The next few days Kath and I were on tenterhooks. If Mum did tell Dad what we had been up to we were not sure; there was no reprimand, and nothing was said to us, but looking in the hovel we found to our dismay the bike had been slung up on some rope, well out of our reach, and harms way, as Dad would say.

With our part of the Common being almost inaccessable except by horse and cart, on horse back, or 'Shank's pony'. Having the use of his nag, Dad's bike was of little use to him, unless he wanted to go to Oxford. To go to Waterperry or Wornall, by the time he had got it out, and pushed it across the fields, it was almost as quick to walk, and certainly according to Dad much easier. So, by slinging it up, it presented no inconvenience, and assured him it would be in one piece if at any time he should need it.

Chapter III

Summer Days

Every now and then mother would come to see us, and stay for a few days. She was lovely; a sort of fairy godmother and beautiful princess rolled into one.

No wonder I loved her, she always smelt so nice, made a fuss of me, and never failed to bring me something in the shape of a toy, or some sweets from Grandma's shop which, I had little knowledge of until after we had moved into Wornall, It was then I became familiar with Grandma and Grandad, and their tiny village shop.

Mother used to say my love for her was only 'cupboard love'. When I asked Mum what this meant, and learned its meaning I remember feeling very hurt that she should think of me in that way. Often I found the only way to express my feelings was to shed a few tears.

Mum assured me that mother did not really mean it – it was only a saying. How complex grown ups were.

Apart from my memories, my greatest treasure from those days, is the old paper mache policeman that mother brought me on one of her visits, with his heavy rounded bottom it was impossible to push him over; he would roll back at me, and I remember crying and being frightened of him upon our introduction.

Possibly that is why he survived so well. Now it stands on the cupboard beside our bed, keeping guard over my wife and I. What a shame it is that so many of our childhood toys become lost and broken, and so lost to posterity. At the same time it gives great pleasure to see some that did survive in the various museums, but to have a relic from one's own childhood days presents an unparalleled joy.

Strange as it may seem, I cannot remember the rainy days of long ago, there must have been some, but I can only recall those lovely sunny summer days down at the Common, life was just one happy round of playing; picking cowslips and cuckoo flowers; chasing butterflies, and making daisy chains, all were prolific in the orchard, which in a way, to one so young was a garden of Eden complete with its abundance of flowers and fruit. Besides my favourite pear we had what Dad called a Blenheim apple and lucious Victoria plums. Even in those days I learnt

the best and biggest apples and pears were always at the top of the tree, making them 'forbidden fruit' for one so young. In addition to this there were dewberries, which grew near to the ground, and within my reach. The blackberries were a different matter, but Kath solved the problem with a hooked walking stick. Then there were the crabapples – everything in its season – Mum made crabapple jelly, and Dad crab wine. Mum's jelly was delicious, but it was some years before I became aquainted with Dad's wine, and was not particularly enarmoured. Although now that I make and enjoy it myself, I wonder if like a good wine, one's taste matures with age.

Mushrooms grew in the next field, and were ours for the picking. Rabbits were plentiful, and Dad often shot one for dinner. Snakes, well, I am not sure if they were ever added to the rabbit stew. I have read the gypsies ate them and have wondered about it. Though the reference to Randall's eels from hedges and ditches from the song, makes this most unlikely.

Once when Jack had been down to the village, he killed one on his way home.

He had somehow twisted it round his stick to carry it, and had dropped it on the garden, just outside one of the front doors, we had two doors, both of them at the front, and facing south.

Although Jack was supposed to have killed it, I was extremely puzzled, because it kept moving and twitching. "Is it dead?" I asked.

"No not yet." He replied, and then added.

"It won't die until the sun goes down."

I kept watch, popping in and out, and reporting its movements, and sure enough when the sun went down, it gave what proved to be its final twitch, and then remained still.

It was gone next morning, naturally I wondered if it had come to life again during the night. I suppose either Jack or Dad had buried it, though I cannot remember if we had rabbit stew that day or not, I have often wondered why Jack bothered to bring it home in the first place. Ah. Well. I suppose it must join part of the list we all have, and become another of those things I shall 'never know'.

Looking back to those early days brings to mind many things that happened, things that were seen, but not understood by one so young.

Once I saw an airship, and marvelled at it, unaware of its significance, or that it had anything to do with the terrible war that Mum and Dad talked about. There was also the instance when Kath took me across the fields, and down the lane to see a set of steam ploughing tackle in operation, totally unaware it had anything to do with the war effort, or that the Government had put an order on the farmer, compelling him to plant a certain percentage of his acreage with corn. Such things were to be learned later, much later. At the time, it was seeing two massive steam engines for the first time, one each side of the field, pulling something that bumped and bobbed along, first to one side of the field, and then the other, turning up the black soil, and burying the grass, all at the same time. Neither did I have the slightest notion that one day, I would work for the sons (Avery Bros) of the man who owned those monsters with fire in their bellies.

Chapter IV

Taught by example

With Kath at school, and Mum nearly always busy, I was left very much to my own devices, dwelling a great deal in the realms of make believe. The old wooden soap box was one of the most universal bits of equiipment of the decade, serving as a table, or when turned up the other way as a cart, as a cupboard when on its side,besides which, it became a mounting block whenever I wished to mount my horse.

When Kath was home, we played houses a lot with her being Mum, and me being her little boy; so naturally when on my own I used to take on the roll of Dad, pretending to do all the things he did such as, cleaning and oiling his gun. I would have a gun one day, and be able to go shooting, but a nice straight stick had to do for the time being, and the timely shouts of 'Bang' served as cartridges.

Most of the things that Dad did, so I pretended to do. Everything he did was perfect, and correct, from dubbing his boots to grooming his horse. Though totally unaware of it at the time; I was being taught by example. No matter if my dubbin was mud, and my horse Prince, Dad's large black and white collie. Prince seemed to enjoy the grooming, and gave no indication that he objected to my riding him except, he would sit down and tip me off when he had-had enough; regardless of how I tugged at his collar he refused to budge from off his haunches. Often I would give up, and start to do something else, only to find he had followed me wanting to play 'catch me if you can', showing this by dropping flat on the ground, barking and prancing, saying 'come on'. I have no recollection of ever catching him, only that it was great fun trying.

Sometimes when Kath felt like it, or wanted to get out of doing something, she would take me out on the swing and teach me nursery rhymes by saying, or singing the words at the same time as pushing me, coinciding the words with each push. I would have to shout them out too. 'Ba Ba Black sheep. 'Dickery, Dickery, Dock'. 'Three blind mice'; and all the rest of them. I was certainly well versed in my nursery rhymes, if nothing else.

These days there is much talk about nursery rhymes introducing violence to the very young. Suffice to say I was more concerned with being able to say them, and what I might get in the way of praise or reward, for doing so than their actual meaning. Surely their original purpose was, and still is, to teach the very young the connection of one thing to another in proportional relationship. The importance of opposites such as 'Good from Bad,' and the exitence and dependence of one upon the other thereby promoting appreciation and awareness.

Nursery rhymes apart, half that infants hear in everyday life is beyond their comprehension, with the other half not holding much interest for them. I was far more interested in what my teddybear would get for tea, and what goodies Mum would be able to provide for us. Bread and jam was a prime treat in those days, with a piece of cake on Sundays only. So no small wonder I had to help Ted out with the little piece Mum always apportioned him.

Living in such an isolated spot meant we had very little contact with the outside world, occasionally Mum would journey to Oxford to do some shopping, mainly to get material to make clothes for the family. Sometimes she walked to Waterperry to see Mrs Baker (Clara), and now and again she would take me with her to see Mrs Shepherd (Lizzy) at Wheatley, alternately they would visit us if the weather was fine, and not too much mud about, a factor to be reckoned with, as they both had to push their prams across the fields to reach our secluded abode.

Apart from them, and Mr Devonshire the old tinker who called every now and then the only people I knew or saw were Mr and Mrs Joey Simmons who lived in the cottages across the pasture, and Mr and Mrs Walter Fonge, and their two sons Ted and Les who lived at Park Farm, the house being a little bit beyond the cottages, and situated at the end of the hard road.

The butcher and the baker, their names evade me, delivered to them once a week, and left our meat and bread at the Simmons's for someone to collect, usually Kath.

Mr Simmons' had lost an arm in an accident and was game keeper in charge of Waterperry Woods; he nearly always carried a double barrelled gun, and Dad reckoned he could shoot as well with his one arm as most could with two.

Once, when I went with Mum to fetch the milk and butter from the farm Les and Ted took me to see their pet lamb, which, having grown quite large was running on the lawn at the front of the house. Apparently, unlike Mary's meek little lamb, it turned out to be a ram, and me being a little one in long clothes, must have presented a challenge, for, sure enough, in about 'two shakes of a lambs tail' he lowered his pretty little head, and bunted me in the tummy, sitting me neatly on my bottom. I think I was too surprised to cry; fortunately I was unhurt, and Ted and

Les grabbed him before he could charge again, it certainly taught me to be wary of animals, especially that particular little – pet. We had a Sunday Newspaper which, with any mail that came for us, was left at Simmons's. There was no radio, so the paper was our only source of news, but the postal service was excellent. A letter cost one penny, and a postcard a ha'penny, with delivery assured next day, anyone intending to visit could give notice, confident their notice would be on time.

One of two other incidents that stand out in my memory, from those

H.R.H. The Prince of Wales
In Robes of Investiture

H.R.H. The Prince of Wales

'early days' was the night an air balloon travelling very low came, Dad said, dangerously close to our house. It was very scarey. The occupants were shouting.

"We are lost – where we are?" Dad went out with a lantern, and shouted back at them.

"Oxford is about four miles to your left, as the crow flies." They shouted their thanks, and much to my relief, were soon gone out of earshot. Dad thought they would not get far, unless they had a lot of ballast on board, as the rope from the basket was almost dragging the ground. He reckoned he could have grabbed it, if he had so chosen. I thought it was a good job he had not done so or it might have taken him away. We never heard if it did come down in the vicinity, so assumed they had a safe journey.

The other incident happened one winter's day when the Oxfordshire Hunt was in our area. There was quite a wide and deep brook running by at the end of our paddock, and spanning it was a rather wide footbridge, just about wide enough for a horse and rider. I learnt later that a certain young gentleman, who was following the hounds, and a lady rider converged on the bridge at the same time; the lady apparently won by a neck, and consequently the gentleman's horse took a plunge into the brook, and flung the young man into the water, soaking him from head to foot so, seeing our house naturally called to see if he could get assistance in drying out.

Mum answered the door, and immediately recognised the young man standing there. It was none other than His Royal Highness, Edward the Prince of Wales, who was studying at Oxford, at the time.

The Prince touched his hat, and said something like. "Good afternoon madam, I have been thrown into the brook – can you possibly help me to dry out?" Mum gave a very gracious curtsey, and replied.

"Certainly sir, come in, I will get you a change of clothing."

Whereupon he came in and sat in Dad's chair, at the same time pulling it a bit closer to the fire, which Mum promptly made up with some dry logs. She was soon up and downstairs with some of Dad's clothes. I think it included his best Sunday suit. Giving him these together with some clean towels she gave another curtsey, and said.

"Perhaps your Highness would like to change by the fire, while Victor and I go into the next room. He thanked her and Mum and I made ourselves scarce.

After a few minutes the Prince appeared at the parting door to show he was dressed, and with a smile said.

"Not a bad fit madam." Mum laughed, and answered.

"It looks better on you than it does on Tom, Sir. "Tom was Dad's name.

She soon got a good blizzy going, and hung the wet togs round it on the big clothes horse. 'Not too close, in case they scorch'. She said. More to herself than anybody. Obviously it would never do to scorch the Prince of Wales's breeches. It was not long before they were steaming, and due for a turn. Mum turned the horse right round, and put the kettle on to the hook over the fire, when it had boiled she made the tea, and asked the Prince if he woud like a cup, to which he replied. "Yes please, I would indeed." Or something to that effect. After leaving it to draw for a few minutes, she poured out, and presented our distinguished visitor his tea in one of her very best cups and saucers, at the same time proffering him the sugar bowl.

I suppose it took about an hour to get everything dried and aired, and the Prince could get back into his own clothes. Mum told me when we were in the other room the first time that he was a real Prince, so I was unable to do anything but stare at him spellbound. Mum said 'it was rude to stare,' but I was in a spell, and unable to help myself – A Real Prince. I suppose I felt very humble, but cannot really remember.

When he went, the Prince thanked Mum very much and presented her with a golden sovereign. Mum thanked him in return, and with another grand curtsey said.

"Goodbye, and thank you again sir." Then we watched him mount his nag, and ride off into the dusk.

We certainly had a lot to tell Dad when he came home that night, besides, we had the golden sovereign to show him, such a Princely Sum, and solid golden proof of our story.

Chapter V

The Move

It must have been the summer of 1919. Circumstances had developed. Kath was leaving school, and would be going into service at the end of the school holidays, and I would be five next year, which meant I would have to go to school. Why, I was not sure, but Mum said so and that was that. Dad, who worked as a drover for Mr Fuller at Town Farm in Worminghall was waiting for a house in the village. Old Mr Veary, a widower had moved into an almshouse. The two bedroomed house he vacated belonged to Mr Fuller, so we would be able to move in.

'So jolly convenient'. Mrs Baker said. She was one of the first of the seventeen children Mum and Dad had brought up, was married, and lived at Waterperry, being grown up she could voice an opinion without fear of rebuke. Everybody seemed to be excited, that is everybody but me. I could see my tiny world falling to pieces. Who wanted to go to school anyway. I certainly did not. Besides, Kath said she would be glad to leave so it was not that good.

Mother came home for a few days – that was good. She and Mum took me with them to scrub out our new house. It was quite a long walk across the fields, but I had been breeched so was able to run about unhindered, and was allowed to carry the broom. Our new house was In a row of four, and the address No 2 Worminghall, Nr Thame. It had a scullery, living room with a kitchen range, a little front room with a small grate to match; the stairs led to two bedrooms, but Mum said. 'We can turn the front room into a bedroom for when anybody comes'. There was a pantry by the back door and a stairhole by, and facing the front door. Each of the four rooms sported a fair sized window that faced south, which Mum and mother measured with a tape measure, brought specially for the job, and which I was given to roll up and unroll just to keep me quiet. I think mother could sense I was not very happy, and tried to comfort me by saying.

"There'll be lots of other little boys and girls for you to play with.

You'll soon forget all about the Common". Here it is seventy years on and I still remember it well.

The floors of the living room, scullery and pantry, were plain quarry

Mother in her Land Army rig toward the end of the
Great War

tiles; the front room floor was ordinary floor boards which, later on proved to be much warmer than the quarries. There were roller blinds fitted at the two front downstairs windows, apparently these formed part of the furnishings, in fact in this case, the only furnishings; they were controlled by endless cords fixed down one side of the frames, and proved to be ideal playthings until I was reminded they were, 'not meant to play with, but for pulling the blinds up and down'. Something I had become quite good at by the time I could see any further action would not be tolerated, so begrudgingly packed it in.

The Scrubbing and cleaning done, the day of no return arrived. At eight o'clock on a Saturday morning two horse drawn farm waggons came to collect our goods and chattels; Dad helped the men with the heavy things, and the rest of us carried out the small pieces. One thing I made sure was safely packed, was the doughkivver. This served as my cot, it was nice and deep with its high sides, and stopped me from falling out of bed, as Mum said. It also served the moment well by holding all my worldly goods in one box as it were. With the waggons loaded, a few outside things left behind, which Dad said he would collect sometime next week; room was made for Mum and Kath to sit at the front of one of the waggons. Dad mounted his nag, and one of the men lifted me up in front of him, and off we went, with Dad's arms one each side of me I felt very safe, perched up so high with my head in the clouds. I was on top of the world – 'King of the Castle', and wanted everybody to see me; being allowed to take the reins, indeed it was me riding the horse with Dad just riding pillion. It certainly was a memorable day the day we moved from the Common down to Wornall, and a completely new world.

Wornall, as Worminghall was commonly called, chiefly by the locals, and those people who were familiar with it, was at the time a sleepy little village in Bucks, situated on the border with Oxfordshire. Sitting in the midst of a green and leafy surrounding with three spinnies, each bounding the one side of three of the four roads leading to and from the village. Townsend marked the Eastern end of the village, and the crossroads, while at the other end the road West passed the Blacksmith's shop, and a row of six cottages, always referred to as 'sixrow', on its way toward Waterperry, another little village smaller even than Wornall, and about two miles away.

I later learned that apart from the Church and Vicarage, the school P.O. Public House; and Blacksmith's Shop, there were three private houses, five farm houses, and fifty cottages The Post Office, was not a separate building, but was operated from one of the cottages by a Mrs Munday. Most of the community relied entirely upon jobs supplied by the farms for its livelihood. The only other industry that existed at that time, was the wood industry, centred in the local woodlands about 2 miles North of the village. This provided a living for about five or six families.

I was in no way concerned with such matters in those early days; the first few weeks in my new surroundings were spent in becoming acquainted with our neighbours, or to be more exact, with Nancy and George Bowler, who lived next door. George was about two years my senior, but being small in stature was in no way overbearing; Nance, as I grew to call her was older than George, seemed to be very capable, and always at hand to advise. She was never lost for ideas, and undoubtedly kept George and me under control, and out of trouble, for most of the time anyway.

One of the first adventures shared with Nance and Camp was that of scrumping. There were some apple trees in the neglected gardens of what used to be No's 7 & 8 which, with the houses no longer there seemed not to belong to anybody in particular. Nance suggested we slip along the field keeping under the hedge, nip through the gap which would bring us almost under the Blenheim tree, and out of view of Wyatts's and Tippings' who lived in No's 5 & 6. This we did, and with me perched on Camp's shoulders the whole operation was quite a success, we stuffed our pockets full and Nance filled the little straw basket she had thoughtfully brought with her. As we made our way back along the hedge Nance said. "Oh dear. What shall us do with 'em? Then added. "We can't et 'em all, and us darn't take 'em home or us'll be in right trouble." I know. Said Camp. "Let's 'ide 'em in the 'edge un 'av a secret store, so us can go un get one when us likes." What a good idea, good ol' Camp. So off we went and found a nice little spot up by the first tree. This was a big elm just up the hedge above our gate; after making a little heap of our bounty we covered it over with grass and undergrowth, very pleased with ourselves, happy in the knowledge that we shared a secret, which, without doubt strengthened the bond between us.

The next Saturday, a week later we decided to visit our secret store for our ration, having agreed that if we only had two or three a week they would last for ages. Imagine our surprise and disappointment, to find on arrival that our hiding place was absolutely swarming with wasps. Camp reckoned. "Millions of the little buggers." Their amount coupled with their intense activity defying us to get anywhere near to our no longer secret store. When we investigated a week later it was to find there were no wasps to be seen, nor were there any apples, 'the cupboard was bare,' apart from cores and skins. We never acted that trick again. Later on when I told Mum about it, she just sighed, and said. "Ah my boy, ill gotten gains will never do you any good." I reflected upon her words, and concluded, with a feeling of shame, perhaps the trees had belonged to someone after all, and that scrumping really was stealing.

Chapter VI

School Time

Christmas came and went, and Easter was soon upon us; naturally with my playmates going to school I longed to join them, so it turned out there was a vacancy in the infants, and I was accepted into the fold, under the wing of Mrs Parsons the 'little room' teacher. The school was situated at the bottom of the avenue, it had just the two rooms, the 'big room' and the 'little room' each with a lobby, which served as cloak rooms with coat hooks, and in each stood an iron stand containing an enamel bowl and jug, in case anyone wished to wash. I think the teachers used them more than anyone else.

Eventually the long awaited day arrived, and it was agreed that Nance should take me, and see me safely home. This suited me well, as Nance would allow me to run and play with the other young ones, and not insist that I kept hold of her hand.

The first few days were wonderful, but like so many others before and after me it was not long before I became disillusioned with the whole affair, and yearned for my freedom. I ran for home four times in the first two weeks. The first time I slipped out of the gate unnoticed, and made it all the way home. Mum was not very pleased to see me, and made it quite clear she was not on my side; after a good scolding she took me by the hand and marched me straight back. From that day on I think they must have kept an eye on me, because the farthest I ever got was as far as the pond, which was about two hundred yards back up the avenue. One of the big girls always ran and caught me, and yanked me back, in spite of my tugging to get away.

From then on I was kept in at playtime, and only allowed out after promising not to do it again. The one and only time I did make it was unintentional, and most embarrassing. Mum had made me a new pair of short white trousers, of which I was very proud, and wearing for the very first time: I was a bit late back after lunch, should have gone before leaving home, but then its always easy in retrospect. The bell was ringing, early I swear; running full pelt I just made it on to the end of the file as the bell stopped. Yes I made it all right.

"Left turn, quick march." Ordered teacher. The sharp turn did it. Splurt! It was running down my legs, wet and warm, and smelling to 'high heaven'. The one in front of me let out an enormous. "Phew!" Almost shouting. "I think Victor has messed himself Miss." Sure enough, by this time the tears were falling. I had well and truly christened my lovely new trousers.

Teacher took one look, saw my distress, and not being prepared to face the unpleasant task of cleaning me up, quietly said to Nance.

"I think you had better take him home Annie." That was Nance's proper name.

"Come on." Snapped Nance. Keeping her distance; so we started the long trudge home, she on one side of the road, and me on the other.

Nancy

All Mum said when we arrived home was. "Never mind, it can't be helped. Worse things happen at sea." So it was not too bad after all, seeing once I was cleaned up, and able to play with my old teddy bear etc for the rest of the day.

Since those days, I have heard of men under shellfire at sea, and doing the same thing. An old naval pal of mine, who survived a bombardment at sea openly admitted he messed himself when in action. He said fear does something to your guts, and affects your bowels, making them uncontrollable, adding. 'If anybody who has been under fire tells you he was *not* scared, then he's a bloody liar.'

On one occasion, when I was a young man a similar thing happened to Dad, but not through fear, he had spent most of the day, and part of the evening at Thame Fair. Had arrived home, was sat down at the table, having 'a morsel of grub', when all of a sudden he jumped up, and shot out of the door, and tore across the back yard to the 'privvy', which was about thirty yards 'across the way'; apparently he failed to move fast enough. Mum and I just gazed in wonder, we had not seen him move so fast in years – if ever, and were not certain what the matter was. I followed him out, and shouted through the closet door.

"What's the matter Dad?"

"I've messed myself boy, its that bloody all-slops." Came the reply. Implying it was the Allsops beer that had caused his predicament. Then, upon hearing me laughing.

"Its bugger all to laugh at." Now over fifty years on I still find myself smiling at this then embarrassment, and the explanation he came up with.

It might be added that 'privvy' was the common word for toilet there were no water closets (W C's) for cottage holders. In the 1920's it was an outbuilding containing a specially designed bucket fitted beneath an elm plank with a large suitably shaped hole, over which one sat. There were no such things as toilet rolls either, the chief bumfodder was newsprint, with tissue paper, so rare, and soft. This reminds me of an amusing little rhyme we used to say referring to the time long before the days of paper.

"When Adam was a little lad,
And paper not invented;
He pulled up grass to wipe his ass,
And went home quite contented."

No emptying of stinking buckets in his day.

I understand it was well into the 1950's before some of the cottage holders at Wornall, and other surrounding villages, were finally supplied with tap water and water closets.

I remember too that Town Farm boasted its own workman's privvy, which was an elm seat similar to the one just described fitted over a deep hole within a small wooden shed with a corrugated tin roof; the thing I best recall is the words painted on the inside of the door, facing the sitter.

"This is no place to sleep and slumber;
But to piss and shit, and fart like thunder."

This was very amusing to we boys, and set us wondering who first wrote it, its origin, and how long ago. In fact I do believe it was signed Shakespeare and countersigned with something that rhymed with jollocks, giving it an eartheness in keeping with its austere and solitary loneliness as it withstood the climatic changes of all weathers, for years and years.

This Town Farm dunikin was situated in home ground, just North of Johnie's pond, and it was reckoned that on a clear day providing the wind was right ol' Jobey's trumpeting could be heard up in the Brickhills three fields away. They knew it was him as he invariably gave a rendering of "god save the king" in perfect timing. One day when a small team of mowers had come together and were taking a breather, old Swelly who sometimes stuttered a little bit, stopped scything and said in a matter-of-fact-way. "Wonder ol' Jobey dawn't bust his f-f-farting clappers b-b-blowing off like that. Then carried on apparently unaware of the amused tittering his perfunctory predilection had caused.

Another story has it that one day when taken short he dropped his pants under a hedgerow, and that one of his farts ensconced within the safety of a skin was, through the force of its own velocity and the aid of a little whirlwind propelled into the top of an eighty foot elm, and hung there for weeks constituting an overhanging threat to the immediate neighbourhood. When it eventually exploded it was thought that the gases, having no definite boundaries had drifted safely off into the upper regions, but nobody could account for the two dead crows found beneath the elm, except perhaps they were roosting at the time of the explosion, and so became the only victims, suffering the consequences of an overwhelming outcome.

Many such tales related by older members of the community would appear to be the outcome of someone's imagination, expanded upon by another's exaggeration, the authenticity of which became wholly in question. Though, living next door, I can vouch for the fact that our neighbour suffered greatly from indigestion and flatulence, and that his mantlepiece was the epitome of a chemists' shelf displaying an array of every patent medicine obtainable from over the counter. Carter's little liver pills; Beecham's pills – worth a guinea a box; Krushen salts that gave you that Krushen feeling; Sidletze powders; Andrew's liver salts; Rennies etc. Undoubtedly Jobey was a type of hypochondriac. Dad used to surmise about the condition of his stomach with remarks like "Lord knows what sort of state 'is guts be in, taking in all that jollop."

With just a single bricked partition wall between us, and our fireplaces backing on to one another, almost every sound could be heard, in fact at times it was almost like living together without the smells; something we were often very thankful for. Being a milker meant that Jobey was an early riser, so complying with dictates he retired around 9.30 most evenings. At 9.00 o'clock all would become quiet next door, indicating they would be sat with the headphones on listening to the 9.00 o'clock news; at 9.30 the kettle would be placed over the fire which in turn would be given a vicious poking. After about a minute the kettle was removed and one could visualise Jobey filling a cup with hot water, standing the kettle on the hob, and then drinking the water with whichever concoction he was currently taking. This was firmly established with the accompaniment of a severe bout of belching and burping, giving the listener next door the impression that every emission of trapped carbon dioxide afforded him great pleasure and relief. For, never once did we hear him say pardon.

Their stairs were identical to ours – eleven treads and the landing. Often as Jobey ascended we would silently count in unison with his seemingly controlled emissions. Purp! One. Parp! Two. Purp! Three. Parp! Four, and so on until we reached twelve which would often be accompanied by an extra loud and prolonged expellation – Bur-Rump! Signalling that would be the last we would hear of next door, combustion wise, until the morning. Perhaps he was subconsciously aware that someone might be listening so that final – Burp-Rump was his artistically crude way of saying. Good-Night! Occasionally he failed to get all the way with his purps and parps, and Dad would say. "The ol' chap must be weakening, he only got to seven tonight." Then conjecture with what sounded like anticipatory hopefulness. "Perhaps 'e's shit 'is self." At other times when he performed well he would credit him with. "Bloody 'ell ol' Jobey's givin 'er some stick tonight."

There were other noises apart from those previously mentioned emanating from the other side of that parting wall. Jobey's son Baggy had an accordion and gramophone to which I together with Nance and Camp, from next door on the other side, was invited to listen. Often Baggy would slow the record a bit and play his accordion to it while the rest of us would sing the words, with one of us beating time on an old tea tray, and Jobey joining in on the spoons. All contributing to what we thought was a pretty wonderful performance. Not so by our. "Bloody miserable neighbours." As Baggy would say. When Dad had had about as much as he could stand, he would bang the back of the grate with the poker, and shout. "Turn that bloody urdy gurdy off, its givin' me the bloody guts ache." Two bloodies, and that was definitely a warning to we visitors it was time to leave, and for Baggy to pack up for the night. Tommy Atkins (Dad) was not a quarrelsome or violent man, but if upset he could be, as Jobey said. 'A rum old bugger.' It was always as well to keep the right side of him; he was an old soldier in the Afghan war; had a double barrelled shot gun, and one always got the impression, if pressed wouldn't be off using it.

One of Baggy's records referred to an old Buffer, apparently a member of the 'Order of the Buffs', and Baggy insisted – every time the word Buffer came into the song it was bugger. Indeed it sounded very much as though he was right, so that particular record together with The Laughing Policeman and Sweet Violets, was played over and over again becoming more and more scratchy as the days went by, and though still giving we young ones a lot of pleasure contributing more and more to Dad's abdominal aches, and vociferous objections.

Chapter VII

Truancy And Deception

After the first two weeks at school, it was sometime before I deliberately stayed away again; although still in the infant class, I doubt if I was quite seven, whether it was winter or early Spring I cannot remember. Across the road from the gate to our cottages was a spinney where all our discarded tins, bottles, and general rubbish was thrown. One day, after dinner, Mum asked me to throw something over the hedge on my way to school. Instead of throwing it I did better and went through a gap in the hedge, really to see who it was at plough in Townsend Ground on the other side of the spinney. Who should it be, but none other than Mo-Ko, that was Herb's nickname; as it happened he was ploughing down our end. Perhaps he was fed up with being on his own all day, but when he drew level to where I was standing, he called "Whoa". To his team, and stopped for a word, which, in broad Bucks went something like this.

"Wha'be up to".

"Nuthin'". I says. "Gooin' to school".

"You dawn't want t'goo t'school. Stop along wi'me, you can 'av a ride on ol'Flower wen us packs up. That was too much; wavering I said.

"I'll get in t'trouble. What 'ull our Mum say?

"She wunt know, if you dawn't tell her." Said Herb.
That did it, he had made up my mind for me. Looking forward to my promised ride I asked.

"'ow long afoor you packs up?"

"Not long us alluz knocks off at three." Then looking at his pocket watch.

"It's purt nigh 'aff one. You u'd be late now anyway. Gee up." He said. So taking hold of the plough handle about halfway down I trotted along, fully committed, and blissfully happy.

Eventually three o'clock came. Herb called his final. "Whoa".

"I reckon us 'av ploughed our acre".

Around the time I played truant

He said. Apparently that was the recognised stint for a two horse team, from seven in the morning to three in the afternoon: We had turned the headland, and set her up (the plough) ready for the first bout next morning. Herb unhitched the traces, rolled up the plough lines, and hooked them over the hames. After tying Flower's bridle to the breeching of the other horse with the end of a plough line, he lifted me on to her back, and being a young man sprang sideways on to the back of the other horse. A couple of clicks with his tongue and we were away, down the headland, out of the gate, down the road, and over the cross' roads into the village. Although our house (No 2) was set well back from the road, we were in full view of the windows.

I hoped Mum would not be looking out, a few more minutes and we were out of sight, and the fear that I might be seen quickly abated. We carried on down the road, pass the blacksmith's shop, and through the gate by the pub which led to the back way to Court Farm where Herb worked. We crossed to the far side of the farm yard to the water trough that was kept filled through the medium of a large iron pump; after having their bits removed, and what seemed ages, the horses drank their fill, swung round together dribbling water as they did so, and without any urging clip'clopped over the cobble stones into the stable, and up to their mangers.

After lifting me down Herb unharnessed the horses, gave them a liberal feed of oats, to which he added a handful of field beans, and said.

The Blacksmith's Shop

"That 'ull make ther' ol'coo'uts shine." Then as we came out, and as he closed the lower door.

"I'll give 'em a good rub down un groomin' when I cums back arter dinner."

We walked together round by the dairy, through the little swing gate, and across Cot'aise, the little paddock that ran up to the road at the bottom of The Avenue. Herb lived in a big house nearby, so we parted company; he to have his dinner, and me to make my own way home, which meant I had to pass the school. Fortunately the school windows were very high up. I slipped by on the grass verge, keeping an eye up to see if anyone was looking out. They were not; so far so good. According to Herb they would soon be out and I would be able to arrive home at about the right time so Mum would not be at all suspicious. I was beginning to wonder if staying away from school was worth the worry, and then who should I meet but Mrs Mare, the parson's wife.

"Hello Victor." She said. "You are out of school early. Have you been an extra good boy?"

Then I told the biggest lie of my life, and so politely too. I touched my cap, and said, as I shuffled round her.

"Yes Mam." I felt really awful, and so ashamed at deceiving such a sweet and lovely lady. I decided then and there that I would never sneak time off from schoool again. At that moment the kids came out, shouting and yelling, laughing and happy, without a care in the world; not like me. Little did I know it, but my troubles were far from over. I ran the rest of the way home, slipped in doors and sat down, just inside the living room door. Mum was sat at her sewing machine facing the window, she was making Dad's shirts, and I hoped as she had promised, some trousers for my Ted out of some of our Jack's old over'alls. Jack worked on the Great Western Railway and was lodging at Banbury at the time.

On hearing me come in she stopped her machine, and looking out of the window, and with her back to me asked.

"Did you have a good time at school?"

"Ah." I answered. She looked round at me.

"Victor, you are telling lies. You haven't been to school. I saw you sat on top of that horse." "Then added. "Windows have eyes my boy". I never forgot that, and always bore it in mind when ever I was up to something I should not be.

"Just you sit on that chair, and don't you move until I tell you.'

I suppose I had only been sat there for a few minutes, but it seemed like hours. I started to wriggle and asked.

"Can I get down now Mum?

"No you can not, and I'll not make those trousers for your teddy bear now." Oh dear, that was terrible; I started to grizzle.

"I'm ever so sorry Mum. I'll never do it again."

"You'll be sorry when you get to school tomorrow my lad." Then added.

"No doubt you'll get the cane, I certainly wouldn't like to be in your shoes." These last remarks seemed to serve the purpose of completing my immediate punishment.

"You can get down now, and help me lay the tea." She said. Perhaps not right back in favour, but I certainly felt a lot better, and anyway, tomorrow was a long way off.

The next morning came, there was no escape, I must face the music. Perhaps nobody would say anything, and maybe I had not been missed. What a hope. It seemed as though everybody was waiting to have a go at me. Apart from Mrs Parsons, my teacher. Miss Goodenough, the big room teacher, and Mr Mare the parson were in attendance. Looking back I think they must have been having quite a game, and a little bit of fun at my expense. They questioned me on what I had been doing during the afternoon. Mr Mare suggested I should have the stick. Miss Goodenough said.

"Do you think we should report him to the attendance officer?"

"What ever shall we do with him?" He really ought to have the cane."

Mrs Parons explained to me that staying off school was called 'playing truant', and was very naughty. Then she said to the others.

"I don't think we should be too hard on him. He didn't really know it was naughty." Then turning to me.

"Did you Victor?"

"No Miss." I answered. Thinking how nice she was, and that I did really.

"Very well, if you promise not to do it again we will overlook it this time.

"Will you promise Just for me?"

"Yes Miss." I said. Knowing quite well I would promise anything to get out of having the cane; it was awful being stood out in front of the class, with them sniggering and all. Besides I would be able to tell Mum I was let off the stick, and so strengthen my case in favour of Ted's trousers.

I got them eventually, but had to wait what seemed to be a very long time before Mum forgave me, and finally made them. They were perfect; just like Jack's over'alls.

SECOND ROW – Eva Tanner, Nancy Bowler, Will Chadbone, Agnes Cross, Joe (Tom) Baldwin, Jack Sparks, George Harman, Betty Tanner & Hilda Baldwin.
THIRD ROW – Cyril Wyatt, Violet Baldwin, Ada Barret, Bertha Cross, Francis Baldwin, Arthur Moore, Annie Chadbone & Mildred Hornett.
FOURTH ROW – Moses Joiner, Milice Hornett, Victor Hawes, Reginald Harman & George Bowler

Chapter VIII

Further Education

My education slowly advanced, I graduated into the 'big room' and standard one, but not all my teaching was gained at school. Living on the other side of us at No 3 was the Edwards' family. Mr and Mrs and their two sons Fred and George. Fred the eldest was named after his father, as seemed to be the expected thing in those days. His nickname was Brusher, how he came by it I know not. George was nicknamed Baggy on account of the nicker-bocker trousers he wore when he was much younger. At the time to which I refer he had just left school, and was working at one of the local farms as a ploughboy and general factotum, and now a man of the world, and very knowledgeable. He certainly knew how to, and was not afraid to swear. I was. Mum told me if I swore the devil would have me, so in my fear and innocence I had always refrained from using naughty words, in fact, I had never found any use for them; that was until Baggy took me birds'nesting round the Ickford road, and started me off.

On hearing what Mum had told me about the devil, he just sniggered, and recited the little verse.

"There was a bloody sparrow;
Sat on a bloody spout.
There came a bloody thunder storm,
And washed the bugger out." Then he said, "There the devil didn't have me. Did he?"

"No," I had to admit. "Say bloody." Said he. "No." Said I. "Go on, you're bloody well afraid to." No I ent." I answered.

"Goo on then. Say it."

"Bl-oo-dy." I dragged out. Baggy laughed.

"There the devil didn't have you; you be still here." Then added.

"Say bugger then."

With gathering confidence, promoted by the fact the devil had not had me, and that I felt none the worse for it, I managed a good round.

"Bugger." Baggy laughed again, then told me another little rhyme.

"Little Robin Redbreast, sat upon a thistle;
Every time it pricked his ass, it made the bugger whistle." No need for

him to say it again. Much to his delight, and my satisfaction. I was able to repeat it word perfect at the first attempt. So my introduction to swearing was well and truly established. Though I took good care to avoid ever letting Mum hear me, or Dad for that matter: Had they known what an influence Baggy was I am sure they would have stopped me keeping his company.

George Edwards – Baggy

Another thing that Baggy and Brusher did, which was against tradition, was to clean their push-bikes on Sunday mornings. Mum strongly disapproved and said. 'Sunday was made for a day of rest', and that they

Worminghall Church

had got six days in which to do such jobs: Whereas, Baggy defended their actions with the remark.

"Six days shalt thou labour, and do odd jobs on a Sunday."

Sunday, according to Mum was also a day of worship, and she insisted that I attended Church at least twice a day, if not three times.

When I first attended Sunday School, Baggy still went although he had left day school, and was working; that was until one sunny Sunday afternoon he was playing with his pocket watch, making its reflection bob around, and land on some of the other kid's faces midst no small degree of giggling.

The Parson – Daddy Mare, observing what was going on, coupled with the mirth, came down the aisle to where Baggy was sitting, and said.

"I'll have that George."

"You can't have that, its mine." Retorted Baggy. And hung on to his precious time keeper that had cost him five shillings.

"Very well, you must leave the class." Ordered Mr Mare. Where'upon Baggy took himself out of the Church, and as much as I and some of the others appealed to him to do so, never came to Sunday School again.

The reverend Mare was a fine old gentleman, and was affectionately referred to by all the villagers as Daddy Mare. He always seemed to be dressed in the same black garb, his waistcoat that held a gold watch and chain had cloth covered buttons he always wore a long black cape hanging from the shoulders, and stiff white cuffs to match his collar, the whole topped by a round broad brimmed hat turned up all the way round that had a shallow crown. He wore soft leather black boots and little black gaiters, and was never without his silver knobbed walking stick. Sometimes he would hold it behind, and across his back held in the crook of his elbows. Some were heard to say, 'this was when he was thinking up his next week's Sermon.' Often he would come to school during scripture lesson, and tell us of his adventures in the Holy Land. That he had eaten unleavened bread, and when he was a young man could fell an ox with one blow.

Mrs Mare was a lovely lady, almost as tall as her husband, who told us he was five feet and ten inches. They had just the one daughter, Margaret, she was about seventeen, and extremely beautiful, or so I thought. She helped to teach we little ones at Sunday School, and if she came near to look at ones drawing, or put her arm round you, that was heaven, but if you could manage to hold her hand after Sunday School all the way to the vicarage, about half a mile, not only was it a triumph over the other kids, it was sheer ecstasy.

I am sure, though only about seven years old, she was my first love. I needed no persuasion from Mum to go to Sunday Schol in those very early days.

With a good view of the school and the Vicarage gate on the right.

The oak gate at the end of the gravel drive, which led up to the vicarage was about the same size as an ordinary field gate, but much more ornate with heavy iron studs, heavy clamp round hinges, and a decorative latch controlled by a twisted iron ring on both sides. The posts were bevelled on their four corners, rebated about nine inches from the top, which was cut four square from there to form a point, all the work of a craftsman. Of course all these details were observed by me at a later date; a much later date when I began to take an interest in carpentry and woodwork.

Those of us who were unable to hold Margaret's or her mother's hand, always ran to hold the gate open for them; often it was already hooked back, but no difference, we used to line up along it, often two deep. Mr Mare would count us with the aid of his stick, often giving us a little prod, say something about the cupboard being nearly bear. "But perhaps you can find them something dear". Then Mrs Mare would say.

"Oh, I think I can." Then off we would go skipping and laughing as we accompanied them up to their front door, whereupon we would all be given a sweet or a biscuit. Often there would be about twenty of us. This was not just one Sunday, but every week. As some grew older, or felt themselves too big and grown up to partake in such proceedings, then others readily came to take their place.

I am sure, no servant of the Church had a more happy and devote flock, nor was there ever a more loved family than Mr and Mrs Mare, and their lovely daughter, not by kids anyway. Even if it was 'cupboard love'.

Chapter IX

Fun And Games

Being one of the infants meant joining with the girls at playtimes; sharing their playground, and their games that were many and varied. They were never lost for a game to play, and were always ingenious enough to find a way to let the little ones join in; often by splitting into groups, with one lot about the same age playing one thing, while other groups would be doing something else, all the time shouting instructions, and encouragement to those of us who were in their particular section. What with the shouts and screams, and excited yells of about forty of us, no small wonder the grown ups said it was like Bedlam when we were out to play.

One of the more popular games we used to play was called 'tig'. The person to start off being tig was selected by a rhyme of elimination. The favourite and the one I best remember was.

"Ink pink pen and ink;

Who made that dirty stink?

Y-O-U"-U being the deciding factor. Invariably accompanied by a loud "Phew!" The person chosen had to chase someone in the gang, and try to touch them, then the touched one became tig, but was not allowed to touch the person who had touched him, or her, before chasing someone else. With all the touch's going on, it could well have been called 'touch' as well, or instead of 'tig'. There were other variations, one being 'touch wood' tig; by touching wood one became immune from being touched, but two people were not allowed to hold the same piece of wood, if they did then the last one to do so was penalised and so became vulnerable.

Another version was 'off the ground' tig-when off the ground one became safe; the only way to avoid the game becoming flat was to run from place to place, and expose oneself to being caught.

Tig was an all the year round game. As were others such as 'pat over the head'; 'queeny', and 'sheep sheep come home'. Queeny was simply a line of children facing the same way as the one who was chosen to be queeny, but about ten feet behind him or her; the idea was to move forward and try to touch the one out front without being seen. If that person turned round quickly and caught someone moving, then they had to go back to the starting line. When someone was able to touch queeny they changed over, and a new game begun.

'Pat over the head' was played with a ball, the players formed up the same as in 'queeny', but the one out front had to bounce the ball, and then as it bounced pat it back behind where someone in the line would catch or grab it; everybody in the line would stand still with their hands behind them, then on the word of ready the one out front would turn round, and try to determine who had the ball, if guessing correctly they changed places.

More fun was engendered if the one doing the guessing brought in a few quips to try and get the one with the ball to give himself away.

'Sheep sheep come home' was another all the year round game. The sheep, usually the smaller ones of us lined up on one side of the playground, and the farmer on the opposite side; the wolf would be stationed in his lair at one side, about half way between the sheep, and farmer, the farmer would then shout. "Sheep sheep come home."
To which the sheep would cry.

"We are afraid of the wolf". The farmer would then shout.

"The wolf has gone to Devonshire, and won't be back till next year; Sheep sheep come home." Then the sheep made a mad rush to the other side, with the wolf catching as many as possible and taking them to his den. The procedure was repeated until all the sheep were caught and eaten unless they were saved by the bell.

Springtime was always 'top time'. The boys would bring out their window breakers; with the aid of a good whip made from whipcord, it was possible to knock a window breaker twenty or thirty yards in a straight line down or up the avenue when going to and from school.

The girls seemed to favour bumbles; these were bigger round and more dumpy than the window breakers, and consequently more static.

Top time was invariably followed by 'trolling-hoop' time; with a bit of stick, and a bit of practice it was amazing the fun to be had during hoop time. The girls and little boys with their wooden ones of various sizes, and the bigger boys with iron ones, rotated by a blacksmith's made hook, about a foot long, and with a handle at the opposite end to the hook which if held towards the bottom of the hoop enabled the operator to reach great speeds, and to beat the school bell.

During the summer months the girls played 'hopscotch' and five stones, plus a great deal of skipping, and all sorts of ball games. While the boys would be enjoying themselves playing marbles; rounders; cricket; catty, and jump on back besides trying to pee over the urinal wall or drown the flies that settled within peeing distance.

Never ever, during my school days did I hear anyone say they were bored; fed up with the confines of school maybe, but at playtimes and out of school there was always plenty of good things to do and enjoy.

Window breaker

Peg top

Bumble

Trolling hoops.

Cricket gear.

Chapter X

First In

Apart from the games described in the previous chapter, one of the most exciting of our summertime pursuits was going down to the river Thame, (which is about a mile from the school across the fields) to bathe, perhaps frolicking would be a more apt description.

In the morning, one of the bigger boys might ask teacher if she would let us out of school a bit earlier than usual, whatever the answer, yes or no made no difference it was arranged we bring our towels with us at dinner-time; especially the first time for the year as the excitement built up to see who would be 'first in'.

We small ones had no chance, but as soon as the class was dismissed at four o'clock, or possibly five minutes to if teacher thought our behaviour deserved it, we took off like long dogs the big boys leading the way, down the road, over the stile through the gravel into Home Ground, across the footbridge and under the wire by the sewer beds into Great Ground, this was a huge field, about a quarter of a mile in length. Those in front would be almost to the far end with the remainder strung out at varying intervals with the smallest bringing up the rear, everybody puffing and blowing and shouting their heads off with cries of.

"Come on, 'urry up." While others would shout back.

'"ang on. Wait for us. There's no 'urry."

Knowing full well they had no hopes of being 'first in' so did their best to make out they were not in the least bothered.

"Anyway our Mum said I wan't to get in if I wus 'ot as it wan't any good to you."

After Great Ground, it was through the rails into River Meadow, and straight down the side of the brook to where it joined the river at what we called Wornall Corner. The Waterperry boys called it Waterperry Corner, but their patch was on the other side of the brook, so our relationship was quite amicable. As a bathing place it was ideal; it had a gravel bottom, and was fairly shallow during the summer months making it safe for the young ones.

I was about six when first allowed to go, then only if the big boys were going, Mum always wanted to know who else would be going. If not sure I always made out – I did, and say one of the big boys names. As far as I remember it always worked, I was never refused. As we got near to the getting in place we started to undress, so by the time we reached it we were more or less starkers, a few more minutes and we were able to join the others who were already in shouting and hollering; splashing and jumping about like lunatics. The warning about 'not getting in if hot' completely forgotten.

Nobody wore costumes, such a thing was unheard of in those days, and our territory was never encroached upon by girls, so to bath naked was accepted as the natural thing to do. Invariably, of those still on the bank someone would ask those already in.

"What's it like?" Never did the answer come back other than.

"A-A-All-right." Or through chattering teeth.

"L-uv-ly." Though often as not it was enough to 'freeze ones balls off' as the big boys would say. One got the impression that those suffering, delighted in inviting others to share their discomfort.

George Harman
"Nobby."

By pulling up, and making a big bundle of reeds that were very plentiful, and by lying across them it was possible to stay afloat and to practice the breast stroke movements. Sometimes the bundle would slip back and tip ones head under, but no matter, a good kick or two would soon rectify matters, and off we would go again.

One of the first things a new-comer had to do was to duck right under; if he failed to duck on his own accord, then the big ones grabbed him and forcibly pushed him under; I found it best to jump in and go straight under, then once they could see your hair was wet nobody took any further notice.

What a thrill it was, the day I first learned to swim. My birhtday being in July, I had just turned seven, and recollect it well. That particular day I was floating along on my reeds doing the usual breast-stroke when suddenly they slipped out from under me, and I was going along on my own. Being able to touch the bottom I waded back up stream then turned round, and pushed out with accumulated confidence swimming with the current to where I could just bottom it again.

Up and down; up and down. I was the last out that memorable day; then could not get home quick enough to tell Mum and Dad that I could really swim. "Well done." Said Mum. "Not bad for seven." Said Dad.

There were no instructors, and certainly no certificates issued; we were all self taught, happy and very capable, but then, it seemed kids were in those days.

One year, I recollect it was a hot summer's day in the middle of a heatwave, and by prearrangement we had taken our towels; some of us had some bread and jam sandwiches for tea, while others had a bottle of water, which we shared, not only in drinking, but in carrying too.

Miss allowed us out a little bit earlier than usual, so off we went to our favourite place to cool off and enjoy ourselves. Enjoy ourselves we did, so much we forgot all about time. Although Nobby's 'old scorched face watch' was hanging by its chain on the single strand of barbed wire that ran all along the side of the river, nobody bothered to look at it. Until eventually Camp thought to do so, and got out to have a look, not only did he find out the time, but discovered our clothes were missing, gone, stolen, only a few towels, and a pair of boots were left behind. Camp let out a yell for all to hear.

"All our bloody clothes 'ave gone." Then it went suddenly quiet, until Widdie shouted. "Course they 'ent, he's 'aving us on." Then cooly asked."

"What's the time?" To which Camp answered. "Half six. Bugger the time you come and see fur yurselves." Whereupon there was a stampede to the bank, with everybody trying to scramble out, and sure enough he was not having us on.

Bill Chadbone
"Widdie."

Imagine the consternation and conjectures, plus some comments which if anything were a bit tearful, with remarks like.

"What 'ull our mum say?" And. "Our dad 'ull kill me." "Besides I can't goo up the village with nuthin' an.'"

By this time we were all out of the river and dry, or drying on a borrowed towel. It was getting a bit chilly, and everybody was really fed up, and looking for a lead from one of the bigger ones. Tucker, who they say got his nick-name when he was little because he sounded his Fs like his Ts, was one of the eldest present. Whether he felt we were all looking at him or not I am not sure, but no general, and no statesman ever made a more famous statement than Tucker when he said. Very slowly.

"I think I'll wrap my towel round my guts un' goo 'ome."

This proved too much for the chaps who had crept up and taken our clothes, and were hiding in the rushes and reeds nearby. They just burst out laughing and came out bringing our belongings with them. Obviously we were all relieved and delighted to get our clothes back and be able to get dressed. Anyway, the culprits were much too big for us to set about. Only a few minutes ago, we were full of despair, and now the clouds had disappeared and we were as bouyant as ever, and able to 'skiddadle' off home none the worse for our little adventure.

As previously mentioned, every year there seemed to be a sort of secret competition to see who would have the honour of being 'first in; 'the year I was nine Camp and I were determined we would be the 'first in' come what may. On Easter Saturday morning we set off down the fields to the river and Wornall Corner. The floods were out, and we had to remove our boots and socks to get through them, and to reach our place of entry.

The river was very high, and being on a corner the current was extremely fast; faster than we had ever seen it before; still this held no fears for us, we could both swim so could not drown. Without more ado we discarded our clothes, and being the tallest it was agreed I should be the first to have his knackers frozen off. With Camp holding my hand I slid off the bank and found the bottom. The cold was terrible, my teeth were chattering, and the water was up to my armpits, but then heroes never complain so slowly I ventured out into midstream and across to the other bank, which was the predetermined goal.

On the way back I faced up stream and attempted to swim, but found the current was much too strong and would have washed me away. I struggled to get my feet down, so gave up the idea of swimming and made my way back to the bank and safety.

I helped Camp in, and being shorter than me the water came almost up to his chin. I warned him what ever he did, not to try and swim or it would wash him away. He was older than me, and thought himself a strong swimmer. Fortunately he made no attempt to do so until he got back near to the bank this side, then facing up stream he struck out, and straight away the current started to take him downstream into deeper water, and although he was swimming frantically the river was winning. Seeing the panic in his eyes, possibly he was too scared and preoccupied to shout for help, I jumped in and by holding on to a small branch hanging down from an adjacent willow I was able to reach his hand, and haul him back to safety.

One thing I know, that that day in March we were both very relieved, and thankful to get out of that freezing water; well aware of the risks we had taken, and resolved not to do it again. I had learned something else from our little escapade, if ever I should get caught in similar circumstances, I would just turn round and go with the stream, until finding a backwater, a fallen tree, or where I could reach the bank and climb out.

The best of it was, after all that the other kids woud not believe we had 'been in'. While Mum and Dad carried on, Mum said.

"You silly little fools – you might have been drowned." Dad said.

"You might have had cramp in that cold water – don't you ever do that again." He need not have worried we had no intention of doing so. Still, no-one at nine years old had done it before, especially as early as Easter Saturday when the floods were out, and it is hardly likely anyone has been daft enough to do it since.

Chapter XI

The Bakers

I previously mentioned Mrs Baker 'Our Clara' as Mum used to say. Bakers lived at Waterperry, and I often visited them on a Saturday, and sometimes staying until Sunday evening, the main intention being to play with Jack and Tom. Jack was my age, and Tom was that bit older, two or three years older, and no doubt had a bit more sense than we two. Although I said play it was more like – doing things than play.

We were always outside, their mum would only have us in for meal times, and to get ready for bed. If it rained we were usually out anyway, and used to get somewhere in the dry. One place we frequented quite a lot was the old carthovel, long since gone. It was a long and low thatched building that housed the waggons from Manor Farm when they were not in use, which in turn housed us, we could lie on their dry beds out of sight of our elders, almost a veritable indoor playhouse.

It was on the opposite side of the road to some thatched cottages, where Blakes lived. There was a big family of them, and just down the road was the Slaymakers, Four girls and one boy, so we were never short of companions. Although most of our time was spent during the Spring and summer in one round of swimming, fishing, rabbiting, bird nesting, walnuting and climbing trees getting young jackdaws and rock pigeons. Most of our past-times and activities were closely related. If it was warm enough we would go swimming, then after dressing do a bit of fishing, we found that where we had been swimming it had disturbed the river bed and so attracted the fish. Sometimes by using dough or cadis we could pull out little roach as fast as we could rebait our hooks, besides perch, which we fished for with worms.

The thing was, we used to shout and holler about, but it never seemed to make any difference, while often, sat on the opposite bank would be a full blooded fisherman complaining that he had not had 'a bite' all day. They could never understand, how we, who were breaking all the rules could succeed where they failed. Of course we never threw anything back except gudgeons; our folks said we could not eat those, though I have read since that people used to fish the Thames for them in the 19th century. Still we invariably had plenty to provide us, and the rest of the family with a good freshwater fish tea when we arrived home, usually as hungry as hunters, which in a way, we were.

If, and when we were fed up with fishing, we would detach our lines from the willow sticks used for rods, and roll them on to runners, throw any surplus bait into the water, and walk round the river searching the willow trees for rabbits. During the breeding season some of the old bucks could be found hiding up in the convenient hollows provided by the trees. Often it was difficult to dislodge them, and I have seen them on occasions jump right out of the top of a tree and make good their escape.

Not many Saturdays passed but what we succeeded in catching one, and often a couple. This type of rabbiting was usually coupled with moorhen's nesting, and duck nesting too. If we were fortunate enough to discover a duck's nest we tested them in shallow water, if they sank we took them home to eat, but if they floated put them back in the hope we could catch the ducklings when they were hatched. The fact that the little devils could swim almost as soon as they were hatched, made that an almost impossible task.

I remember that once we took some duck eggs home, and put them under a setty hen, she brought them off, and Jack reared them for the pot. When they feathered up we had to catch them one at a time, and one of us cut one of its wings while the other held it, and so cut short any attempt they might make to fly off to their natural habitat, because they remained absolutely wild right up to the very end of their short lives. As I remember there was nothing better, and nothing we liked more than duck stew, with a good hunk of home made bread.

Regarding moorhen's nesting, if there were only up to six eggs in the nest it was safe they had not started to set, if there were seven or eight then we would test them the same way as the duck eggs. Just one egg was never taken, because she would forsake the nest, if it was the first layed; and if a bit later in the season it would be sure to be addled, and unsurpassed as a stink bomb. More than eight it was pretty sure they were inedible; if there were about sixteen, and one was light coloured, it was the last layed and safe to take home for breakfast.

Jack Baker and I were great pals, and all our weekends together were spent happily exploring the surrounding countryside; we knew of every gap and way through or over the hedges; where we could get over the brooks and ditches without getting our feet wet. We knew just where to look for all kinds of wild life, often we would find a rabbit's stop, and get the babies out when they were runners and play with them, then put them back and go on our way looking for something new to do and without a care in the world.

One Saturday we two went off egging all round the brooks and ponds, and came back home with thirty-two moorhen's eggs. We refused to share them with Jack's brothers and sisters, Charlie, Patsy, Tom and Dorothy. Bob was the baby so didn't really count. Thirty-two between six was not going to work out too well, so we tried to justify our greediness by pointing out with great emphasis, we had been to all the trouble, got ourselves stung, scratched and 'wotchered' (wet footed) whilst they had done nothing towards it.

Mrs Baker fried, first one sixteen, and then the other and we ate the lot between us. I think it put me off moorhen's eggs for ever to say nothing of the guilt and shame I still feel at the recollection of our inexcusable greediness.

We used to wander the fields and lanes freely, birdsnesting, violeting, wooding, blackberrying, and down the woods primrosing and nutting. Nobody took any notice of us nor we of they, though we were always a little bit dubious about gypsies, and kept our distance in case they carried us off, little realising they would not want more mouths to feed. Never did I hear of, nor can I recall a reported case of child molestation in any way, much less sexual assault or murder such as we read and hear about in these modern times. True we children were never allowed to read newspapers, not that we would have wished to, nor have had the time to spare if we had been.

Jack Baker

I was quite happy with my weekly comic 'Puck' and my 'Tiger Tim Annual'. One of which is still in my possession. There was ever the option of a swap with one of the other kids. As I grew older Baggy was always good for a Sexton Blake or a Fu Manchu. 'Blood and Thunder'. Baggy used to call them. I used to like 'Tinker' Sexton Blake's assistant.

Wherever we went we always shut gates, kept out of standing corn, and were never cheeky to grown ups. In the main we avoided crossing mowing grass, but kept round close to the hedges; very often we would see a cast sheep and turn it back to its feet, see a cow calving, and run to tell the farmer, or one of his workmen where she was, often this meant the difference between a live or dead calf, and a copper or two to us.

Sometimes in our travels we would see where a courting couple had been rolling down the grass, and would be amazed at the area affected. Some of the bigger boys used to look round to see if they could find a johny, sure evidence that they had been 'at it'. Whatever that meant.

There was no such thing as sex education, but even at an early age we knew quite a lot about nature. Wornall school was next to a farm yard, and we would often watch a cow being bulled, or a mare being covered. Great big shire stallions were led round the villages specifically for that purpose; then there were the pigs, goats and more often the dogs to be seen mating, so country kids had quite a spattering of sexual knowledge. There was always the clever ones who knew all about it, or thought they did.

Although we knew there was something went on between mums and dads, we never really knew just what until we were much older. It was none of our business anyway. Here's a little jingle we used to say.

"Mummy and daddy went down to the wood;
Daddy said he could do mummy some good;
Mummy layed down, with daddy on top;
And daddies old belly, went flippety flop."

Then there was the tale of one of the kids coming to school and saying to another one.

"Did you know you could eat candles?" Then adding.

"Well, you can, 'cause last night I heard our dad say to mum, blow the candle out dear, and let's have a little bit."

I well recall when about seven, sitting on the grass verge with a little girl of similar age, who shall remain nameless;* who suggested it I cannot be sure, but we agreed to show dicks. "I'll show you mine, if you show me yours." I showed mine first and thought what a fine little fellow he was, but when she showed hers there was nothing to see, just a little crack. I said, thinking hers would be like mine.

"Where is it then? I can't see it." To which she replied pulling the leg of her draws over a bit more.

"Thats it. Can't you see it? You must be blind."

Still I could not see one, and found it rather puzzling, being my first object lesson in the difference between little girls and boys. A bit later on one of my mates who had a little sister, explained it all to me, and persuaded her to show just to satisfy my curiosity.

* 'A gentleman never betrays his lady.'

Chapter XII

Outings

Back in the 1920's there were very few outings for anybody who lived, and worked in the midlands. Much less for children. Mainly because they were unaffordable, and the coast was upwards of a hundred miles away. Still, to go to Oxford or Thame to see the shops, especially around Christmas was really wonderful. To peer into the window of Miss Jones's toy shop at Thame, and to decide what one would like for Christmas or birthday was indeed a treat. Not that one ever got it, but it was nice to dream and hope until those very special days came around, and though disappointed there was always next year to look forward to. Mum used to say.

"We must wait and see what next year brings." Inferring that something might turn up, though resigned to the fact it never would.

There were only three major outings in my childhood. The first was a visit to Regents Park Zoo, when about seven, with aunt Liz living near to it, it was convenient for mother and me to spend a while with her and my cousins. This apart, the most outstanding features were the journey by train, and the behaviour of the monkeys on 'Monkey Hill'.

The next was a visit by train to the wonderful Empire Exhibition at Wembley, which everyone was talking about, and the papers were full of. This was with the school, I suppose it was considered by the authorities most important that children over a certain age should be made aware of, and to learn all they could about it. Anyway I know Miss Goodenough, our teacher was in charge, and that we had brown bread and butter with pineapple chunks for tea. I remember too that she was not very pleased with me; not ever having brown bread before, I didn't go on it a lot and said.

"It looks as though it's bin dropped into a dirty puddle." I was quickly told, in no uncertain tones. "Eat it or go without." Being hungry I ate it, and found it was not too bad after all. Just two things other than the tea, remain in my memory; one was the 'Red Indian Chief' who in all his regalia stood with arms' folded at the main entrance. Would have liked to stand and stare, but there were more important things to see, and we were bound to have to write about it all on our return to school after the holidays.

At the seaside Worthing 1924/5. From left to right Mrs R. Cross, Mrs H. Mare, Mrs E. Bury behind Mrs P Bury, Mrs G. Hawes, Mr George Hawes, Mrs F. Chadbone & child, Mrs J. Neil, Moses Joiner, Mrs J. Loyatt, Bertha Cross, Reg Harman, next two not known. Mrs W. Joiner, Mrs F. Veary, Agnes Cross, Rene Joiner & Kit Sparks.

The other, and most impressive thing of all was nothing to do with the exhibition, but the news placards, and the paper sellers shouting.

"Accident to the famous jockey – read all about it." Apparently, the famous jockey was Steve Donoghue, who had been injured in a racing accident that afternoon. The hustle and bustle of that evening in London stayed with us all for a long time and remained an evergreen topic of conversation for many a day that followed.

The next and only other outing during my school days was a journey to the seaside at the age of twelve. I, like most of my chums, had never seen the sea. Waterperry school organised a day trip to Southsea, and being a friend of the Bakers and a regular visitor to the village it was arranged for me to join the party for the fee of ten shillings. So I stayed overnight with my pal Jack to make sure I caught the bus in the morning. No danger of that, we were up with the lark, ready and full of expectations, impatiently awaiting the arrival of the bus, fearing it may have broken down, something they were most susceptible to. Finally it came, and we scrambled aboard all vieing for a window seat, but Jack and I sitting together agreed in a civilised manner to take turns.

Off we went with our packed lunches; all agog and looking forward to playing on the golden sands we had all read and heard about, and to paddle and possibly swim in that lovely warm blue water.

Our first stop was Winchester Cathedral. Am not sure, but I think it was Reverend Todd who officiated the tour of the building, pointing out the architectural features, and to tell us a bit about the flags which adorned the walls. Not that we were particularly interested, our main object was to get to the seaside as soon as possible.

Waterperry School Group 1923
Back Row: Dorothy Grimes, Lucy Slaymaker, Ted Fonge, Thomas Baker, Esmy Coles, Olive Slaymaker.
Middle Row: Patsy Baker, Ada Joiner, Edgar Blake, Dolly Soanes, Jim Soanes, Charlie Baker, Lottie Slaymaker.
Front Row: Harry Blake, Basil Grimes, Ron Slaymaker, Edward Soanes, Jack Baker, Margaret Slaymaker, Will(widgy) Blake
Very Front: Joan Fonge, Dorothy Baker.

At last we arrived. What a let down. What a disallusionment. Not a grain of sand to be seen anywhere, nothing but big pebbles which hurt our feet as we attempted to paddle in the smelly old sea water. Jack and I agreed it wasn't a patch on Waterperry cum Wornall corner, and our very own river Thame. Strangely enough I have never hankered for the seaside since then, and often wonder if that first visit had something to do with it. Anyway none of us were disappointed when we were moved on to Portsmouth, and taken aboard Lord Nelson's Flagship – 'Victory.' We found this much more interesting inasmuch we were able, on seeing the blood stains, to conceive in our imaginations, some of the action that took place over a century before, at the same time concluding that like their admiral what brave and wonderful sailors they must have been; not forgetting the poor little 'powder monkeys' who would have been about our age. Actually thanking our lucky stars we were born when we were, and not back in those cruel days when men, and boys, were compelled by a pressgang to serve in the English navy, when perhaps what we thought of as bravery was really the recognition that wasn't alot they could do about the situation they were in, but to fight like hell for survival thereby committing acts of bravery in the quest for self-preservation. As Jack said. "I'm bloody glad I didn't live in them days." If Jack did not say it. I'm sure like me, he must have thought it.

Reverend Todd and Mr Morris (head gardener at the big house) at the planting of a tree near to the old granary Waterperry to mark the Coronation 1937 with many of the Villagers in attendance.

Chapter XIII

Law And Order

Our village was situated centrally, surrounded by Ickford, Waterperry and Shabbington, out wider Brill, Long Crendon, Oakley, Stanton St. John, Wheatley, Tiddington, and a bit further afield, the other side of Thame was Haddenham, where it was said.

"They thatched the ponds to keep the ducks dry, and put a leg out of the window to see if it was raining."

Although there was little evidence to be seen there always prevailed an undercurrent of hostility between the villages; especially between us and Ickford. Our favourite little jingle, ever ready to voice if any of the Ickfordites were in the vicinity was.

> "Brill on the hill;
> Oakley in the hole;
> *Dirty* little Ickford,
> And pretty Worminghall."

Usually, the arches between our respective villages were considered by the young to be the borders; if the boys from one side ventured across after the girls from the other it was at their peril, the home crowd usually out-numbered the visitors by two to one, and forcefully persuaded them to beat a hasty retreat. On reflection, there were very few marriages between the Wornall and Ickford societies. We used to call Ickford kids. "Ickford Shags'. Often chanting.

> "Ickford Shags;
> Come to Wornall to pick up rags;
> To make their mothers' puddin' bags."

And there was great jubilation if our cricket team managed to beat theirs, which, I must admit was not very often.

They were considered to be a cunning, cockey lot, from Ickford. They had a Chapel, we didn't. They had two shops, and two pubs, while we only had one of each. The one thing not begrudged them by us, was their village copper, though in all fairness, I never heard a bad word said about Mr Snelling, the first one I remember; not so his successor. His name appropriately enough was Climber. Dad said. 'He would do anything to gain promotion, even pinch his grandmother.'

Ada Barrett on Waterperry Arches, her cycle spanning width of lane 1932.

One day a little gang of we boys was sitting on the rail at Townsend, the general meeting place, perfectly happy, minding our own business, when the new copper, P.C. B....Y. Climber came up to us and dismounted his bike – you could have heard a pin drop. Then he asked with menace in his voice, so I thought.

"Which of you is Moses Joiner?" Moey said.

"Me Sir."

"Right, what's this I hear about you; throwing bricks at people's doors? Window tapping, and dropping dead cats down old folk's chimneys?" To which Moey replied looking at me.

"No, we didn't do that, did we ol' man?"

Of course, I confirmed Moey's answer with a tremulous. "No."

"Oh! So you're one of them, are you?" Said the copper, looking my way. I felt for a brief moment, quite pleased to be part of the adventure. Then he continued.

"Which would you rather have, a good hiding by me, or go to Brill?" Brill was the local police station, and we all dreaded the thought of being taken there, and being locked up, besides just think of the disgrace it would bring to our families.

"A good hiding sir." We said in chorus.

"Hmm! He snorted." You wouldn't when I had done with you."

"Don't let me hear anymore reports, or you'll all be for it." If you cop us, then we'll cop it. I thought, perhaps that's why they call coppers coppers.

On another occasion; the Sunday before bonfire night, the youth of the village was congregated as usual at Townsend. Dad used to say they were a lot of hooligans, and for me to keep away from them, but if I had the chance I would sneak off and join them. I had done just that on that particular Sunday afternoon. Some of the chaps had fireworks in their possession, and of course, true to character were letting a few off amid shouts of.

"Stand well back, and watch the lightning flash," Just as a 'Little Demon' went off sure enough, round the corner came P.C. Climber. Some dived through a gap in the hedge, and ran for it. Most stood their ground. I managed to keep in the background, and hide behind some of the big ones.

"Who was good enough to let that one off?" Demanded Climber. There was no answer.

"Very well, if no-one owns up I shall report the lot of you." By this time he had unbuttoned the flap of the top pocket of his tunic, and removed a notebook, not taking his eyes away for one moment. Everybody's eyes including Climbers turned straight to Baggy. I thought at the time it was a mass betrayal, although he was the culprit, we had all enjoyed the fun but were quite willing to sacrifice one of our mates to save our own skins. Poor Baggy, he had no option, but to admit his guilt.

"It was me," He admitted. I felt quite proud of him, thinking how brave he was. "Right, name and address." After Baggy had told him, and he had noted it down, he added.

"You'll be hearing more of this." Jumped on his bike, and rode off, up the Oakley Road, leaving us all a bit dazed and nonplussed.

Sure enough, after about a week Baggy received a summons to appear at Brill magistrates court charged with 'Discharging a firework on the King's Highway on the Sabbath, and thereby causing a disturbance.'

Subsequently, he was found guilty and fined 5/-, just five sevenths of his weekly wage. And to hink what the youth of to day gets away with. Its conduct often attributed to the times we live in. Indeed the times that have been allowed to develop through laxity of discipline, and the withdrawal of sufficiently severe deterrents by the authorities, to say nothing of the disregard for religious teaching, not only shown by the authorities, but by many parents who shrink from the moral duty of sending their children to Sunday School to learn right from wrong, and good from evil.

Sometimes the crimes committed by the young are so base and evil, one cannot but feel they are unaware, through ignorance, of the enormity of their sins. 'Lord forgive them, for they know not what they do.' Can in many cases apply equally to both parents and offspring.

All credit to my foster parents and teachers. They taught me right from wrong, and the Ten Commandments. Mum used to say to me. 'If you go into someone's house, and see a pin upon the floor, pick it up and lay it on the table – not put it in the lapel of your jacket. Never take anything that belongs to someone else, no, not even a pin.'

If at any time in later life I did wrong or was dishonest. I could not plead ignorance, I had been taught the right way, and if I transgressed it was my own doing, generated entirely from freedom of choice.

Let me hasten to say, I am no stranger to the violation of law. In the army my dogma was. 'Regulations and rules are for nitwits and fools.' To break the law of the army, was punishable by the law of the army; and so it is with the laws of man the punishment does not always fit the crime, especially in this present day society of ours.

P.C. Climber built up quite a reputation, and at the same time kept law and order within reasonable limits. He certainly encountered no more trouble from we young ones. The mere thought of what he might do to us, together with dread of the 'birch', and the 'cat of nine-tails' was sufficient deterrent to keep us on the straight and narrow, and out of serious trouble.

Chapter XIV

Ways and Means

Most of the adult inhabitants of the little village of Wornall, who were living there during my childhood, scraped a meagre existence from off the land; just as there forefathers before them. They never seemed to to 'rush and tear,' but always kept 'steady on.' The majority were pious to some degree, and accepted their lot in life; had but few possessions, knew the only land they would ever own, would be the six feet alloted to them in the Churchyard, just as would their masters, a thought that must have given them a certain amount of satisfaction.

After tea and ready to start carrying again. The rades around the top of the waggon indicating an elevator was hitched to the rear of it. L to R Will Baldwin; Fred Chadbone; Agnes Hawes; relations' of Polly; Polly, Will's wife; Matilda Hawes. Not sure of the lad – looks like Norman Turner?

The usual wear was corderoy trousers, with bell-bottoms and flaps, held up with leather thonged braces and a wide leather belt, with leather straps buckled just below the knees, these were known as 'Yorks', and allowed the wearer to bend without having to keep hitching them up, especially when using a reaping hook. Besides making most of her own clothes, including those lovely white linen aprons, which, then boiled and starched were unsurpassed for whiteness, Mum also made Dad's shirts with shirting supplied by Capes of Oxford, also his vests of flannel from the same source. His 'Long Johns' were purchased from F.G. Hawkins of Thame.

A jacket and waistcoat of hard wearing material, possibly tweed, a neckerchief and cloth cap plus woollen socks and hob-nailed boots completed his outfit, the whole of which was purchased with the money gotten from overtime during haymaking and harvesting.

"Dad's waistcoat housed a silver watch and chain, purchased through the post from Graves' of Sheffield. Later on when we bought a wireless from the same firm on instalments, he would check his watch with the six o'clock time signal and declare "They be 'alf a minute out with their signal tonight."

To suggest it might be his watch, would be out of the question and be courting a derisive blast.

Only but a few of the farm labourer's jackets were not lined with a deep poacher's pocket; not that they were habitual poachers, but it was very convenient if they happened to strike a rabbit in its form when walking across the fields in the line of duty, or, when going to and from their place of work. Not many employers objected to their workmen taking the odd rabbit or swede, and not many workmen would do so without permission. I never heard of anyone being sacked for stealing; to keep such a thing secret in such a small community would have been virtually impossible.

The wage of a carter in the mid twenties was twentyfive shillings. A cowman was payed about a florin more than a carter or a stockman. Everybody lived from 'hand to mouth'; there was very little left over for beer and baccy, or anything else, after the rent and the coal for heating, paraffin and candles for lighting, (there was no electricity) plus the victuals had been payed for.

Times were indeed hard, especially for large families. Clothes were handed down; at odd times one pair of boots had to do for two children, meaning they could only attend school on alternate days until a new pair could be bought, which meant going to Thame or Oxford, or the Tallyman called with another pair, ordered on his previous visit. All items were payed for on the 'never never' at so much a week, according to what the housewife could spare, so understandably most people were never out of debt. One thing we always had plenty of was water, all free, either drawn or pumped from a deep well, pure, clean, fresh and cool, with no water rates to pay. We kids drank gallons during the summer months, ran everywhere we went, were as fit as the proverbial fiddle, and as skinny as herrings. With plenty of water flushing away the impurities aided by a dose of epsom salts, every Friday night whether we needed it or not. Little wonder we were rarely ill.

We were for ever being told that water was good for us, and it was what 'made lions' strong'. No coke or canned drinks; fizzy lemonade was sold at the pubs, so too were crisps, but these were beyond the reach of kids, unless they were given as a special treat at feast time, or a visiting uncle or aunt felt magnaminous, which was not very often.

Cobbling was an acquired skill of different degrees attained by the majority of fathers, who were forced by circumstances to have a go to try and save a few coppers. Sixpence saved was sixpence made, making it available for a more demanding purpose. Practically every farm worker rented a plot of allotment at a nominal rent of sixpence a pole. He could not really afford not to; ours was a sixteen pole piece, so with the ground that went with the cottage Dad managed to keep us in potatoes and greenstuff.

All but a few managed to keep a few laying hens, while most kept a pig in the sty that was supplied together with a hovel and privvy to most of the tied cottages. The aim being to have the pig killed for personal use. Some would keep two; one for the market, and one for indoors, the one being sold payed for the other, making it free except for the labour which was discounted. October was the usual pig-killing time. Round about that time the farmer Dad worked for used to get a truck of coal in, let his workmen have it at cost price – 10/- a ton, he also allowed them the means of haulage to cart it home from Tiddington railway station, we always had two tons of coal, so with about four hundred weights of potatoes, and two sides of bacon, we were set up for the winter. Dad used to say every year.

"Well mother, we've got plenty of taters and bacon, and plenty of firing so we shan't starve, nor freeze to death." This always seemed paramount in his mind, and even now in these times of plenty I recall his words of the twenties, and stock up with fuel and potatoes, with the thought of strikes, and the possibility of a hard winter uppermost in my mind.

True, we kept seven or eight hens, but the only time I was allowed an egg was at Easter as a special treat. Most of the time they were sold to Mr Blane the eggler from Crendon, with the money spent on butter or anything from off his cart that Mum needed. Of course, whenever big brother Jack came home on holiday, or for a week-end he was given bacon and two eggs for breakfast, besides fried bread, tomatoes and sliced potatoes. When I asked Mum why it was Jack could have eggs, and not me. The answer I got was.

"Because he goes to work."

"He's not at work now." Says I. "He's on holiday."

"Don't you be cheeky my boy, it doesn't become you." Said Mum.

"And anyway he's a man, and needs eggs, you don't you are only a little boy; when you grow up you'll be able to have as many as you want."

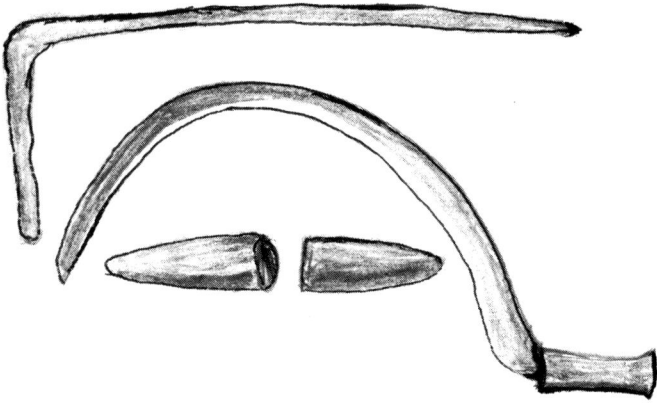

When you grow up, the times I heard that.

'Can I stay up Mum?' When you grow up you can stay up all night – if you want to.' Would be the answer. Its no surprise kids always want to grow up, little do they know of the disallusionments that awaits them when they do, how lots of things they wanted, and wanted to do will not mean a thing later on in life. I well remember declaring. 'When I grow up I'll have as much paste on my bread as I want – half a pot or more.' Like so many other things in life, once a hope or desire is realised it seems to lose much of its wonder.

'When you get a bit bigger was not so bad; I was always getting a bit bigger so was ever hopeful; folks used to say. 'Doesn't that boy grow fast.' Unaware that I was always stretching up to get tall. The only way I got new clothes was when I had outgrown, or worn out my old ones. With boots, a pair of hobnails lasted about three months, after two or three mends.

Dad often said he never knew how I could 'scort' them out so fast, when he could make a pair last two years. He never kicked an old tin up

the road or every loose stone he saw, in fact, everything kickable I had to kick, it was sort of compulsive; every puddle I came upon had to be stepped in. Then there was always the pond on the way to and from school. I always felt compelled to step in a bit farther than anyone else, and then swear blind I was not 'wotchered' (wet footed). He reckoned I would get my feet wet in a desert, that I would manage to find water somehow, and certainly never die of thirst. The only time he ever clouted me was when we were sat in front of the fire one evening, he in his high backed Windsor arm chair, and me on my little stool. I still have it to this day.

I used to take my boots off, and put my feet on the fender in front of the hearth to try and get my socks dry before Mum asked me if they were wet so I could say no, and so avoid a scolding. It was a bright steel fender, and damp socks would send it rusty. That particular evening, Dad woke up from his snoozing, and saw my socks were steaming. I think Mum must have been out in the kitchen. Anyway he said.

"Get yur fit off the fender boy, yur socks be wet through." I knew I ought not to say it, but I did.

"You've got yours on it Dad." Wham! His great big hand caught me over the ear and knocked me clean under the table, where I lay bawling and sobbing for some time, until I was brought out by the threat of bed.

"Ah well, you shouldn't answer me back my boy." He said.

"It'urts me more than it'urts you." My ear was still singing, but I believe it did, he was genuinely upset, and no matter how much I deserved it he never hit me again. The nearest I came to it was when I broke his sharpening stone. As usual I was out in the hovel making something; needing to knock a nail in I looked round and there was just the thing; grasping it by one end in my right hand, and holding the nail with my left I gave it a couple of little taps so it would hold on its own. Then gave it a good clout right in the centre of the rubber. Oh dear, it broke clean in half. I felt quite sick. What should I do? Put it back where it was with both ends together, perhaps he'll not know it was me. What a hope.

Sure enough that evening Dad decided to go grass cutting. Mother came to see us that day, and I was indoors with her and Mum, when we heard Dad shout my name. "Vic come 'ere."

"Better see what he wants." Mother said. I knew what he wanted all right. He was just coming out of the hovel, with his 'hokey pokey' in his right hand, and the broken rubber in the other.

"What do you know about this?" He demanded.

"I was only hammering a nail in." I replied.

"I'll give you hammer a nail in." He said, as he made a move in my direction. I scooted straight indoors to mother and sanctuary.

"What's the matter." She asked. On telling her, she said.

"You go and tell Dad you're sorry, and that I'll pay for a new one." I felt a lot better on hearing that, and nipped off to where he was cutting the path, along by the gooseberry bushes. Keeping a safe distance I said.

"I'm sorry Dad, and mother says she'll pay for a new rubber. "Whether it was my apology or mother's promise to pay, or a combination of both I am not sure, but something wrought a change over him. He gave a little smile and said.

"All right my boy, thank 'er very much." Then went on with the task in hand. I strolled back indoors, hands in pockets whistling 'I'm for ever blowing bubbles.' Thanking my lucky stars mother chose to visit us on this particular Thursday.

Mother – about the time I broke the sharpening stone.

Chapter XV

Visiting

Sometimes Mum would send me up to the shop for something she had run out of. The village shop was kept by my grandma, but aunt Matilda usually attended to the serving. I would always try to manoeuvre my visit to coincide with teatime, which, with all the farming fraternity was five o'clock. This meant grandad arrived home a few minutes after five, and might see me, or if not, and he was home, and could hear me, he would call to aunt Matilda. "Is that young Vic out there?" Followed by.

"Send him in." Where upon I went through the scullery, always referred to as the backhouse, and into the living room commonly known as the fronthouse. The furnishings were quite simple, but practical. Coconut matting covered the large red quarry tiles, a rag rug lay in front of the small kitchen range; an arm chair on either side of the range, one of which was grandmas' being a lady's Victorian button-back. Recovered and resting in my sitting room today. A sixfoot long rosewood table ontrestle legs; four Windsor kitchen chairs; an upright piano, a chest of draws and a grandfather clock completed the simple equipage.

Grandad always found time to talk to me, and consider my childhood wants. "Give him a piece of cake." He would say to aunt Matilda or grandma.

"Help yourself to scratchings." To me, or.

"Would you like a bit of bread un'lard?" There was always plenty of that to be had at home, but not much cake. If I ever found the courage to ask for a second piece on a Sunday teatime. Dad would say.

"No. You can't. There's plenty of bread un' lard if you be 'ungry.

Sometimes grandad took me with him when he visited his old friend George Tipping. (Gerry) who lived in a thatched cottage down beyond the pub, across a little meadow and a footbridge with a handrail that I could only just reach, and which caused me concern, lest I might fall into the deep ditch below. Their greetings toward each other, were usually in the same vein and vernacular.

"Good marnin' Garge." "Good marnin 'Manywell." Then one or t'other would say

"'ow be gettin' an?" With the other answering.

"Mawn't grumble, I suppose, 'ow be you?"

"Got the screws a bit, reckon us 'ull sun get a fall."

Gerry was a kindly sort, he had a lovely long beard and side whiskers, was tall, and like grandad wore a 'Baden Powell' type hat, or trilby; cords, and identical to Gerry only, a long sort of frock coat. Often he thrust his hands behind him, underneath the tail of this and lean slightly forward as we did a tour of the garden and orchard.

Looking back I have concluded his appearance was a facsimile of an Australian bushman. His whole demeanour gave the impression he was wise, steadfast and reliable. No surprise he and grandad were good friends, they were certainly birds of a feather.

I recall one day we were walking round, the trees were covered with apples, with quite a few on the ground, and Gerry saying to me.

"You can pick a'apple up, if you wants one boy." Which I reluctantly did, thinking I would much rather have been allowed to pick one of the low hanging ones from off the tree. Undoubtedly the disappointment being conducive to my remembering the incident so vividly.

Some years later, my uncle Vic related a story to me about Gerry, which depicted his character to the full.

When digging postholes, he and Tom Honour dug up a tin of sovereigns. They split them equally, and decided to keep their lucky find a secret, but Tom failed to keep his mouth shut, and 'let the cat out of the bag.' Consequently the police visited them to consficate their find as 'Treasure Trove'. Tom gave his up, but Gerry refused to surrender his, for ever insisting.

"Guts 'ad it, guts must suffer." Even when the police came with a horse and cart to take him to Brill, and into custody. He still insisted.

"Guts 'ad it, guts must suffer." Implying he had blown the lot on booze. The police, somewhat frustrated, ordered him our of the cart and never bothered him again.

The sequel to this little story is; George Hawes the then carrier at Wornall, (grandads brother) took the sovereigns, a few at the time to Oxford, and changed them for him, and when Gerry died at the good old age of eighty-two. The sum of eighty pounds was found beneath his mattress, reputed to be the amount of his share of the find, and more than enough to pay for his funeral.

With only fifty cottages in the village, everyone, not only knew everyone else, but all were familiar each with the other, their ways and habits, for whom they worked; there likes and dislikes, in fact, practically all there was to know. Camp's mother was a nice little lady who always gave we youngsters, some of her gilly flowers to go in our May garlands, and being well aware of our limitations lent a helping hand in their construction. In keeping with tradition, we always aimed at finding some may blossom for our garlands, but were never allowed to take it indoors, because it was supposed to be unlucky.

To we kids there were a few very important days in the year. Mayday was one of them. With our garlands prepared the previous evening, and put in water over night, we had an early call, and did a tour of the village before school, visiting the farm houses and any others we thought likely to come up with a penny or two for our efforts, presented by our garlands and our unrehearsed musical rendition. With everything arranged we always managed to get to school 'on time' after usually spending a few of our coppers on the way on liquorice and sherbert dabs from aunt Tilda's ha'penny box of goddies.

Worminghall Post Office

Some of the people we visited on May morning often requested we sang one of the songs we had learned at school. Mr. Sammy Moore 'always asked for 'Ye Banks and Braes', and would make us go through it until it was to his satisfaction. He always rewarded us with a penny each;

seeing he lived opposite the school there was little risk to our talents being over strained as the first bell rang at five to nine, we ran across the road ready for the line up, and the day's slog.

The introduction of May Day as a holiday by the Labour Party came about fifty years too late, and for the wrong reasons.

Such people as Sammy Moore apart, the May day song we sang at the door of every house we honoured with a call was, to the best of my recollection as follows:-

"Good morning ladies and gentlemen,
We wish you a happy day;
We've come to show our garlands,
Because it's the first of May."

"Welcome, welcome lovely May.
Breath so sweet, and smile so gay;
Sun and dew, and gentle showers,
Welcome, welcome month of May."

See the web the spider weaves
Round and round the lupin leaves;
Merry birds are full of glee,
And so's the busy little bee."

"And children are as glad as they,
To welcome in the first of May;
Come sister come, away, away,
And you shall be the Queen of May."

Aunt Matilda

*Picture advert that used to hang
in the village shop*

Chapter XVI

Without Aitches and Gees

Although Baggy's dad's name was Fred, everybody called him Jobey, not we young ones, we were brought up to be respectful to our elders, and though we might refer to him as Jobey, never to his face or within the hearing of someone who might rebuke us. Indeed Mr Edwards' was quite a character, and enjoyed great prestige as the local mole-catcher. Besides that, if a wasp's nest was discovered, he was sent for to dispose of it.

On looking back one marvels at the system he used, to do just that, and how it was there were no tragedies; one can only conclude that neither he nor anyone else was aware of the risk and extent of danger promoted by the use of potassium of cyanide. He placed it at, or just inside the mouth of the nest, the wasps dropped dead as they left or entered, then after a couple of days, he came along and dug out the comb and destroyed the grubs. Very effective, and descriptive of the obedience of we kids who were told not to touch or go anyway near, simply by the fact we all escaped disaster.

An amusing little story concerning Jobey, stands out in my memory. One Sunday Mrs Edwards decided to wash the peas she had podded for dinner under the pump; she had them in a colander, and was slowly pumping a trickle of water over them. Seeing this, Jobey took the colander from her saying.

"I'll show you 'ow to wash paes Missus."

Whereupon he held them under the spout and gave the handle a terrific pump. The force of water washed them all right – right out of the colander all over the brick surround of the pump.

"Well done fool." Said his Missus.

"Now you can pick 'em up." She added as she stomped off indoors. Fortunately for Jobey, we the young onlookers helped him, so the only loss was Jobey's face, plus a few peas we helpers managed to slip into our mouths' unobserved.

Back in the twenties we were taught to speak properly, to do so though seemed much harder and long winded than the way we communicated with each other when out of school, and away from anyone likely to correct us. It seemed that as soon as we were out of the class room it gave us licence to disrupt our very limited vocabulary, and lapse into a language made up of almost nothing but disjointed monosyllables. When meeting a friend the greeting – might well have been.

"Hello. How are you?" It never was, instead it would be "'Ow be an." Much more simple and to the point.

All aitches were considered superfluous, not that anyone said so, but the dropping of them was proof enough, if on the occasion they were used, then often it would be in the wrong place. For example. Jimmy Kirtland once said to Mrs Hoddinot, the farmers wife.

"The frost 'ad all my happles Mrs 'Oddinot. No doubt the lady smiled inwardly, but thought none the less of Jimmy because of his lack of education. He was a successful small-holder, with a milk round, and a wood business, which was all the more credit to him seeing that he had very little schooling of any description; not like we young ones, we were always being told how lucky we were to be getting an education.

"Not like we wuz, alluz at work." They would say. Rarely did we say 'yes'. It was always. 'Ah!' When asked isn't the day long enough to say yes? 'The answer would invariably still be.' Ah.' More in defiance than anything.

Jim Moore – road mending.

One never asked an acquaintance.

"Where are you going?" Just.

"We-er be gooin'?" Or. "We-er be to?" Often the reply might well be.

"No w'er much, we-er be you?" Then possibly an agreement would be made suitable to both parties, and they would travel together, or separate ways if neither could think of something to do or somewhere to go, which was not very often.

One day I had joined up with Squidge, one of my mates, we were some bit away from home round the Waterperry Lane, when we bumped into Jimmy Moore the roadman, and were greeted with.

"Wha'be you young buggers up to?"

"Nothin' Mr. Moore.

"No I'll bet. cum eer an' let me giv-ee a stripe, if you dawn't deserve one now, you sun 'ull. Squidge slipped round one side of him, and me the other. Not the vestage of a smile, nor a word until we had run well out of range, only then did we laugh, and call him a miserable old bugger, making sure he was unable to hear us, in case he told our dads.

As the aitches were dropped at the front of words so were the gees at the end of any word ending 'ing, such as; going was always gooin'; being bein'; seeing seein'; doing doin, and so on. We never said. 'I am not', or I haven't,', but, I 'ent', I'ben't, or I'ant', the same as in aunt. Don't was always 'dawnt'. Will not or won't, was always 'wunt'. I will, was, 'I ull', The simple exclamation. 'I'll do it.' Was further contracted into. 'I'll dut.'

Other words in everyday use were 'ockered and accull'. Ockered being a corruption of awkward, but often meaning – pretty upset, and accull indicating it will, or will not work. When a process whatever it might be was judged to be practical or otherwise the term.' It wunt, or, it ull accull was used. Hence I dare, this possible derivation put into rhyme.

> 'Ere's a very simple fact;
> If it wunt work, then it wunt act;
> But, if it ull act then act it ull,
> And so we get the word – accull.
> viz., it is acculling; it acculls; it is accullable; it
> acculled.

Besides specific words there were lots of little stories involving the way country people spoke. One I recall was. The ploughboy to the ploughman, as they sat under the hedge eating their lunch. 'That's a big bit of cheese you've got sir.' To which the ploughman replied. 'No, that ent chaze boy, that be swade.

> Something else we used to say.
> "Be I Bucks? Be I .....b'aint;
> If you dawn't throw our bawl

Back over that ther' wawl;
Us wun't 'av a bawl a'tawl a'tawl."

Then there is the time honoured one of when the young girl brought her boy-chap home to Sunday tea, and in spite of her charge for all to be on their best behaviour at teatime. Mother calmly saucered her tea, and said. 'Chap, or no chap! Sasser my tay I ull, un burn my chops I wunt.

Another one I remember was about the little boy and his dad putting in fence posts. Time was getting on and the boy tired and fed up. When the dad said. 'One moo're boy.' To which the lad, cheered with the thought of packing up and going home to mum, asked. 'What then dad?' Only to have his hopes dashed with the reply. ' Another Bugger.

The words 'gret and girt' possibly from the word girth were used in the graduation scale of greatness. When describing something someone had seen, Most likely a cock and bull story anyway, they might start off with 'twas a good un'. Followed by, 'twas a big un,' then a girt big un, 'graduating to a', bloody gret big un. 'Culminating in the final superlatives of.' The bloodiest, girtest biggest cock, or bull, or whatever it was they may or may not have seen.

Supposedly this broad Bucks'slang survived up until the second World War, which in a way disrupted the village communities, with people joining the armed forces, evacuees being billeted, and servicemen from far and wide intermingling with the country folk, all with a degree of influence, helped together with the B.B.C., to standardise a sort of creditable English we could all understand. Although some of the old lingo lingered on.

In the mid thirties, I had taken my girl friend home for the first time, who later became my wife I might add. Dad and I were discussing gardening, when referring to something in connection with it, he said.

"You no caw tut." After a while, as young couples used to do we decided to go for a walk, there were no cars in those days not for us anyway. After we were alone and the first of the kisses over. Her first words were.

"What did he mean by, 'you no caw tut'?" I had to laugh, it never occurred to me she had no idea of its meaning, so I explained by putting the sentence into its correct pronunciation, purely and simply.

"You have no call to," Meaning in that context. "You are not obliged to."

A short while ago I tried out the same expression on my teenage grand-daughter. She looked extremely puzzled as well she might, after explaining it to her she shook her head, and looked at me a bit curious like, or so I thought.

Although the war destroyed a lot of the old Bucks' slang, all is not lost.

Often I visit some of my old friends of childhood days, and still some of them who have never left the district incline toward that old way of speaking, and I find myself slipping back into it with them, thoroughly enjoying their company, and sure that if I should live to be a hundred I would never lose my countrified accent, nor, would I wish to do so.

One word I have never heard anywhere else; having asked people from all over if they know its meaning, the answer has always been in the negative. The word is 'wotchered' meaning wet footed, not only is it coloquial, but it seems it is confined to the little villages of Wornall, and Waterperry only.

Another word that seemed to be exclusive to Wornall was 'Butty'. Apparently a corruption of Buddy, often used loosely between males of all ages. An adult might use it to a young one struggling to do something by saying.

"You'll at to 'av a bit moor puddin' afoor you can do that ol'Butty," Invariably ol'preceded Butty irrespective of age, it was a sort of substitute for mate, indicating a bond of friendship existed between them.

To be one's 'But' was really something, only your best pal was your But, instead of greeting him by name one would say. "Woot o' But." Or. "'Ow be an But?"

Another word in common use was 'athurt'. One never went across a field or anywhere in fact, it was always 'athurt' followed by the name of the field, such as. "Athurt Gret Ground." Meaning. "Athwart Great Ground." Not ever having to write it, it was some years before I realised it was a corruption of athwart, being so natural and commonplace in its everyday use that its etymology was never in question.

Coming back to "Butty"; I always thought it to be a corruption of the Americanism, Buddy. Then on reading an old book published in 1885, I discovered a "butty" was a collier who had a 'stall" in a coal pit; an apportioned space from which he could quarry coal, being paid for each ton brought to the surface. He employed three or four men to work for him, he himself labouring with them, but with the responsibility for the proper working and safety of the "stall".

On relating this to an old friend who came from a mining area and worked in the pits as a boy. He was able to confirm it, and to add that a "stall" was part of the coal face which was referred to as the "stable", and that "butty" was often used as a term of mate or partner, inasmuch he can remember that when playing at marbles or darts with a partner and someone made to go out of turn, the expression was often used. "No! It's not your turn, 'butty can't follow butty". Meaning a player could not follow his mate who would often be his best pal, as it was common, and still is, for pals to partner each other in games of the times.

On further research I was delighted to find the word "Butty" in an old dictionary; the definition being, – a chum, comrade, esp, one who takes a contract for working out a certain area of coal, or a partner in such., ns Butty-collier; Butty-gang. Indicating this was originally a provincial word, and that it was brought south by people moving out of the coal pits, possibly in search of a healthier and less hazardous way of life. Such as my old friend Derick whom I now call "Butty".

Vic & Win's courting days 1936

Chapter XVII

Blood And Tears

Living on the verge of the village was marvellous, we were in the real country as soon as we stepped outside the gate, or slipped through the post and rail fence at the back of the pigstys; we used to play cricket and football in the field out back. At the top there was a pond where we could, and often did play 'dick-duck-drake' by throwing and skidding a stone over the top of the water, saying a word each time it bounced. Dick duck drake buy a pen-ny cake. Not often anyone got to cake, sometimes Baggy did, but with we younger ones it was usually just dick duck.

They say Sir Wallace Barnes got the idea of the bouncing bomb from playing the same game when he was a lad.

One day we were playing merrily away; Baggy pulled his arm back to let fly, when somehow Camp's ear got in the way, the edge of the stone caught it. Camp let out a yell, and suddenly the scene changed from joy and laughter to one of blood and tears. Nance took a little hanky from up her knicker's leg, and tried to stop the bleeding.

There was no consoling Camp, he was bawling his head off, I had never heard such a row.

"We 'ud better take 'im 'ome." Baggy said. It was quite a little way down the field, but we scuttled along, and Camp eased up a bit with his bawling, which in turn eased our anxiety, that was until we got nearly home, then he let rip as loud as ever. Mrs Bowler heard the racket, and came to meet us.

"What ever's the matter?" She shouted. Baggy explained the best he could emphasising he 'couldn't help it'.

"You should be more careful." Responded Camp's mum. Then taking hold of Camp's hand give it a little snatch.

"You shouldn't play with the big boys, I've told you before." This little rebuke did the trick, Camp stopped his bawling, his mum took him in to clean him up, and when he came out a few minutes later to show us where it was cut we had a job to see it. Our Mum said.

"He was more frightened than hurt." That was the end of our dick duck draking for a little while.

There was just one thing I wanted more than anything else for my eighth birthday. In fact more than I had ever wanted anything before. That was an airgun, a Diana, they cost just five shillings; not much these days, twenty five pence, but a tremendous amount in those days just to satisfy the whims of a nipper. True I could catch spadgers in a mousetrap baited with a piece of bread, or in a brick trap that Taggy had shown me how to make and set, but that was not half so exciting as stalking them with an airgun. I knew, because I had been up Moey Joiners', and he had let me have a go with his; it was great fun.

People would go mad if they saw an eight year old with an airgun these days, but nobody took any notice then except for a precautionary word now and then, such as.

"Mind we-er you be pointing' that thing, that 'ud blind anybody if it went in ther' eye ya' know." The same with shooting birds, nobody said we should or could not.

The sparrows and starlings were nothing but a nuisance, they were always round the hen runs stealing the hen's grub, The blackbirds were not much better they stole the gooseberrys' and currants. The thrushes were different, they helped to keep the snails down so were spared the bullet. We used to say a little rhyme.

"Robins and wrens,
Are God's best friends;
Swifts and swallows,
Are God's best fellows."

Under no circumstances would we ever dream of shooting any of those. Well, one day, when up at Moe's I did shoot a robin by mistake. The leaves were on Chadbones' apple tree. Seeing a sparrow fly into it I crept up and could just see part of it through the leaves, took aim, fired and

down it came, on to the garden near me. I was crouched down behind some greenstuff so was hidden from the windows.

What followed next was the quickest ever interment of a robin, on record. I scratched a hole in the soft soil, pushed the warm little body into it, and covered it over, all within the matter of about two seconds.

Going back up round the houses, Mrs Chadbone was there to greet me; she must have been looking out of her window.

"Did you shoot my robin?" She demanded.

"No. Mrs Chadbone." I replied. 'Butter wouldn't melt' attitude.

"Well, you shot somethin' I saw it fall.

Reg Harman (Brewer) on parade.

"That wuz a spadger. "I countered." Fortunately I had just previously shot and killed a sparrow, so was able to show her it. I could see she was not fully convinced, so kept away from Moey's, and stayed out of her way for a week or two. When I did see her again she challenged me with.

"Hi! You little devil, you did shoot my robin, I 'aven't seen 'im since that day.

"No I didn't Mrs Chadbone, one of the cats must 'uv 'ad 'im." I suggested. Moey said later. 'That's wot I told 'er 'ol'man, she made out if it want you it must uv bin me. I sun told 'er it want me." Then added.

"She ent'aff ockered." Although she never really knew what happened, she certainly had a good idea, and never quite forgave me. I was always 'that little sod what shot her robin'.

With my birthday getting nearer, my pestering for an airgun became more and more persistent. Finally Mum began to weaken.

"Your mother's coming next week, I'll see what she sez." That was it, I was halfway there, if Mum didn't mind, then I was pretty sure mother wouldn't. Sure enough, when mother came and I was able to state my case it was to a sympathetic ear. She had no objection as long as it was all right with Mum. So it was arranged I would get my airgun. That little victory gave me my first inkling that if one wanted something bad enough, and tried hard enough, one stood a very good chance of getting it.

Like so many other things in a young person's life, my airgun became, as Dad would say, 'a five minute wonder.'

After a few weeks the novelty had worn off, perhaps not so much worn off, but that I had considered myself graduated to a No. 1 shotgun. Moey had one, he was a bit older than me, and his big brother Jock had bought him it for his birthday, it fired a little cartridge that made a good bang, which was most pleasing to the ears of we 'big game hunters'.

Anyway, I decided to sell my airgun to Brewer, he kept on about it, so in the end I agreed to let him have it on trial, and if it was any good he would give me three shillings for it. No worry about that, I knew it was all right, so I let him take the gun, and gave him about twenty slugs for the trial. Next day, he greeted me with.

"That airgun ent no good ol' man." I was flabbergasted.

"Of course 'tis, anyway, 'twuz when you 'ad it.

"I know it ent." He continued.

"I can 'old my 'and in front on't." I couldn't believe my ears.

"Right." I said. "Let's see ee do it."

"I'll show ee at dinner time." He retorted.

At the time he was living with aunt Betsy, not my aunt but mothers', we always referred to her as aunt Betsy. She was Brewer's granny.

Come dinner time we ran up the avenue to his place. He had no slugs left, but I found a couple in my pocket. He went indoors and brought out the gun. Aunt Betsy stood in the doorway and watched proceedings. Brewer put in a slug, cocked the gun, and held one hand in front of it, and pulled the trigger. To my amazement the slug just trickled out of the muzzle.

"There I told ee twant no good." He said, as cunning as he could be.
"What 'av you bin at with it?" I questioned. "You'll at to pay for it."
"I ant done nothing' with it." He answered.
That was it. Brewer's old granny let rip at me. Like an old wolf defending a cub she was.

"That thing ent no good, ee ent paying for that; you get off with it, if it wuz any good ee ent 'aving a airgun anyway, them things ent safe so sling y'ur 'ook, and dawnt let me see it 'ere agen." Phew! After such a tirade there was not much I could to. I grabbed the gun, and fighting back the tears ran off home to tell Mum. All she said, and very quietly too.

"You'll learn my boy."

That night I dismantled the gun and found some little bits of wire nail inside the barrel. Obviously he had cut a three inch nail up into little bits with a hacksaw and used them as slugs, and so jammed it up. I managed to get it working again, but it was never so effective as before I let Brewer have it on trial. Of course, when I tackled him the next day he swore blind he had done no such thing.

Yes I was learning all right. What blooming liars some folk were. I told him so too, rather hoping he would start something. For that moment I really felt like giving him a bloody nose, but it soon passed, and we were soon very good pals again.

Chapter XVIII

Taggy Tater

How he got the name of Taggy I know not. Very few people have two nick-names, but those who do must surely be something out of the ordinary. So it was with Taggy, his real name was Tom Chadbone. Chadbone was a fairly common name in the locality, and undoubtedly in those days of large families, most of them were related.

His other nick-name was Tater, tacked on to him through a remark he made at school during a discussion on foods. Something was said about potatoes being a staple food, and Tom piped up with. "Ah! I likes taters, us ets a lot uv them." Everybody burst out laughing, and from then on he was known as Tater as well as Taggy.

There was another Taggy in the village – Taggy Tipping an elderly man, so to differentiate between them, the question would be asked, which Taggy? Taggy Tipping or Taggy Tater? Old Taggy or young Taggy? Not that the question often arose; its hardly likely old Taggy would catch sparrows in a brick trap, then hold them on a chopping block, and poleaxe them, using a stick with a nail driven through it about an inch from the end. That is what Taggy Tater did. He used to say.

It is alleged – "That ent cruel, that's 'ow they kills cattle." Someone said that once he stuck a wheat straw up a frogs behind, and blew it up to such an extent that it busted. I like to think it not true, and if it was, he was so repulsed and disgusted with himself, he never resorted to such behaviour again.

Taggy was about twelve or thirteen when I was eight or nine. He seemed a big chap to me, and was always looked up to by we younger ones.

Anything new in the way of games, you could bet Taggy introduced them, whether he invented them or not is in question, but he was always coming up with something. He made a steam roller out of an old treacle tin and a piece of faggot wire by making a hole through the centre of the lid, and another opposite in the bottom, then thread the wire through, replace the lid joining the ends of the wire on the outside leaving enough space for the tin to spin round, tie a length of string to the wire, and pull it along; before long every boy in the school had one. Tater was not satisfied with that he soon had about six, all connected up, riding 'piggy back,' some turning one way, and some the other.

The next move was to fill the tins up with stones and dirt, pull them through some water, either in a ditch, or the pond, so when pulled along the road they made a good rattle, at the same time leaving a trail of muddy water in their wake.

This success, as with all Taggy Tater's successes, would be acclaimed with a couple of extra loud, 'Nunc Goo's' he got from reading 'Pip, Squeak and Wilfred.

Another of Taggy's inventions was to make a hole with a hammer and nail in the middle of a cocoa tin lid, thread a length of string through the hole with a knot to stop it pulling right through, then by holding the end of the string, and running along the lid would rotate on its edge. Unfortunately the string soon wore through, but Tater soon overcame that by using a short piece of wire at the tin lid end.

Tom Chadbone (Taggy Tater)

This warranted a few more 'Nunc Goo's'. Nobody could do a 'Nunc Goo' like Tater, nor anything else for that matter. His noises were something to be heard indeed; possibly it was something to do with adenoids, but he could certainly make the most horrible rows.

One day he asked my friend Widdy and I to go wooding with him, Widdy was a bit older than me about the same age as Tater. His proper name was Bill Chadbone, probably Tater's cousin. He also had two nicknames, the other one was 'Titu' which he got when he was a little one, apparently he was being bullied, and said. 'I'll Titu' instead of. 'Kick You'.

When we were first approached to go wooding, we were not very enthusiastic, it was Saturday afternoon and wooding seemed to be a waste of good playing time.

"I got to goo un get our mum some sticks to boil the kittle for tay." Explained Tater.

"Tell you what, we ull take the ol' pram un I'll give ee both a ride round the lane. That sounded better. "Aw right." We agreed.

"Bags fust ride." I chuckled in anticipation. Tater nipped round his back and fetched the old pram. The shade was missing, the body was knocked about a bit; it had done service for four young 'uns so Taggy Tater reckoned.

"A lot better than 'avin'to carry the 'ood in a sack." Widdy opined. With a few brr-ums Taggy pulled her up by the bank, I hopped in and away we went hell for leather, swinging and swerving all over the place, just missing the bank one side of the road and then the other. I clung to the sides, laughing and hollering, occasionally holding my breath and shutting my eyes. Widdy was running behind shouting it was his turn. Just as we got to Hancock's corner a motor was coming. We were going too fast to stop so Taggy took evasive action, hit the bank, shot me into the ditch, and fell in on top of me; there we lay much too weak with laughing to move until Widdy came and gave us a pull out.

The old pram was upside down on the bank with the wheels spinning. This gave genius a bright idea. "I know." He shouted. "Turn 'er upside down over that gutter. I'll get underneath 'er, you turn the wheels un I'll be y'ur barrel organ." No sooner said than done. Taggy crouched down in the gutter – the rainwater trench dug by the roadman to allow the surface water to drain off the road into the ditch.

Widdy and I, amid much laughter lifted the pram over him; he was completely hidden. We started to spin the wheels, one of which was squeaking, and he started to make his music. Well music, never did we hear such a row, no, never since, nor ever will we than that cacophoney made by Taggy trying to imitate a barrel organ.

We would hardly turn the wheels for laughing, we were both so preoccupied we failed to notice the approach of Miss Harvey the private nurse from Thomley Hall, until she came level to us, and jumped off her bicycle, asking, in a very refined voice.

"Have you tipped the baby out?" Widdy and I were trying to tell Taggy to shut up, but to no avail, our banging and shouting only seemed to stimulate him into further realms of discord. No wonder the good lady thought we had tipped the baby out, more like a nursery of them by the sound of it. Finally Widdy regained enough composure to answer her.

"No Miss, we are playing barrel organs."

"Hump!" She exclaimed, as she tossed her head.

"Pity you haven't better things to do." So saying she hopped on to her bicycle, the saddle showing up the fat cheeks of her backside as she pedalled away from us, and round the corner out of sight.

Better things to do, she said, that reminded us of our objective. Not a stick of wood had we collected. Hurriedly we lifted the old pram from off

Taggy, and told him what had happened.

"Nosey ol'bugger." Was all he said, then as an after thought.

"It's no odds to 'er what us does." "I know what she wants!"

"My turn for a ride." Demanded Widdy. "You're bloody welcome." I answered.

"Come on then." Shouts Taggy. "Hop in. Any more for the skylark." In jumped Widdy, and away we went nonstop to Thomley corner and the spinney. Those two went through a gap in the hedge, and into the spinney to throw the sticks over into the road for me to load into the cart; to which the old pram had suddenly changed. I had to keep my eye up, now and then I was forced to dodge a flying object, such as a rusty tin. That bloody Taggy would act anything, then swear blind he hadn't done it, or that it was an accident.

I remember one dark night there was quite a gang of us; Ticky; Prinny; Sam; Camp; Squidge, besides some of the younger ones, and of course Taggy, all running behind the carrier's cart, trying to get up on to the tailboard to grab a free ride. Being the biggest Taggy was up first. The next thing the rest of us knew he had his cock out, and was pissing all over the rest of us. Laughing his bloody head off and shouting.

"Cum an you lot, urry up it's startin' to rain." Then loosing off the loudest of farts. "It's thundering too." We couldn't help laughing at the dirty bugger. Later on it was agreed unaminously. That was the warmest rain, and the smelliest thunder any of us had ever experienced.

In spite of his tricks, it was a sad day for we boys of Wornall when Taggy Tater's family left the village and moved High Wycombe way. Somehow there never seemed to be so much fun after he had gone.

Some ten years later he came back with a mate, and camped for the weekend round in George's ground. Widdy, Camp, Squidge and I joined them and had a great time, recalling and talking about past incidents most of the night; enjoying a drink and a sing song, with Taggy, who we now called by his proper name – Tom, playing the mouth organ with great skill; confirming to us that growing up had added to his accomplishments, and at the same time indicating he was one of those chaps who could do almost anything, and do it well.

That was the last time our paths' crossed, what happened to him I doubt if I shall ever know, but I do know that knowing him contributed to my full and happy memories of long long ago.

The steam-engine has supplanted the stage coach, but it has not succeeded in driving the carrier's van off the road, nor do we think that the motor 'bus, which snorts its way along the lanes in many districts, and tears up the road into the bargain, will succeed where the railway has failed.

We confess to a liking for the slow but certain steadiness of the carrier's van, not so much as a means of conveying passengers as merchandise, and as yet the country carrier is indispensable. He flourishes everywhere, and in country towns one sees the vans from outlying villages drawn up in the market square while the carrier bustles about on his various errands.

Time has made but little changes in the carrier's van, which is the same old lumbering vehicle the country over, going at the same jog-trot pace, and the carrier of to-day is but a modern edition of the worthy who did duty in the time of Dickens.

Everybody knows the carrier; everybody trusts his memory; and whether it is a parcel to go into town or one to come out, the country dweller falls back on the carrier. It is difficult to say what the town tradesman would do without the vehicle which never hurries and yet is generally in time, and the country carrier is only human if he chuckles to himself when he passes a motor hung up by the side of the road and cheerily offers to give the passengers a lift.

It is said that the 'bus driver and cabby in London is threatened by the motor, but it will be a long time before the latter supersedes the country carrier.

TERMS MODERATE.   ESTABLISHED 1872.

G. HAWES,
Carrier,

WORMINGHALL, THAME.

THAME: Tuesdays and Fridays, "Fighting Cocks," 3 o'clock, for Worminghall, Ickford, and Shabbington.

OXFORD: Wednesdays and Saturdays, "Anchor Hotel," New Road, 3 o'clock, and Victoria Coffee House, St. Clements, 4 o'clock, for Worminghall, Waterperry, and Holton.

All Goods entrusted to my care will receive Prompt Attention.

HORSE AND CART FOR HIRE.

Authorised Agent for the Native Guano Co.

The carriers cart at Worminghall was finally replaced with a motor-bus in 1926.

Chapter XIX

Cow Minding

One of the few ways the young lads of the village could earn a few bob was to do a bit of cow minding for Jimmy Kirtland; being a small smallholder Jimmy had limited pasture land, some of which he had to conserve for making hay, so was obliged during the spring and summer months to supplement this by letting his small herd of milkers graze on the wide grass verges, along the Oakley Road, and Maul's Road, both of which led into the village. After milking and school time, Camp was one who took on the responsibility of minding Jimmy's herd, which entailed keeping it out of the traffic's path, and making sure no cow strayed off the verges on to private property.

There was very little traffic to worry about, so with but little to do Camp was always glad of a bit of company, which I was often willing to give.

One of our pastimes would be to find a suitable piece of ash stick with which to make a whistle, or whittle with our pocket knives.

In the Spring we busied ourselves bird's nesting, and often got a fire going, half filling a treacle tin with water, and boil the eggs we had managed to collect; such actions would be frowned upon to day, but was accepted as normal in those days. We kids always being out of doors, were always hungry so a few bird's eggs became a welcome supplement.

By what I can remember Camp got two shillings a week for his chores for Jimmy together with an occasional pint of milk, and a few eggs if Jimmy or Mrs Kirtland felt extra generous, which was not very often. Two shillings was 10p in today's money, but was a lot of pocket money for a lad then; whether Camp was allowed to keep it all or not is in question, there was very little evidence that he was.

In spite of Jimmy's ungenerous ways, he was for ever surrounded with a number of we boys who, were always being manipulated into giving a helping hand at what ever he needed doing; haymaking, wurzel grinding, chaff cutting, faggot loading or stacking. His secret was to keep up a sort of entertainment by telling stories and singing little ditties, which we lapped up, he was a master at parodies, and no one could tell a better or more convincing tale than he.

Even now I remember him telling us that when he was a young man, he worked at a farm, and after a cow had calved how he got round the young dairymaid to give him some curds and whey. Adding with a wink.

"The Three 'erberts"
Moses Joiner (Moey) Reginald Harman (Brewer) and Victor Hawes (Jack above Water)

"Of course, I'd curdled her a few times."

If one of us did something a bit daft he was open to ridicule by the rest of the gang, but Jimmy would come up with a tale about somebody doing something dafter, so the current happening was soon forgotten.

We boys loved him, and I must say learned a lot by keeping his company, such as how to hold and use a hay fork, a shovel and a billock, besides much of little value, but what did it matter? We were happy, and so was he in getting his odd jobs done for nothing.

When issuing the chores Jimmy's endeavour was to keep us apart as much as possible. Regarding the estimated value of boy labour, he used to say.

"One boy, a good boy;
Two boys, 'alf a boy,
Three boys, ne'er a boy at all." How right he was.

He used to call Moey, Brewer and me. 'The Three 'erberts. One day he said.

"Of course, you three be second cousins, and there ent much between 'e. I reckon if I wuz to put 'e in a big 'nd shake 'e up, there 'ud be no telling' who 'ud cume out fust." Then laughed and suggested one or t'other of us. I'm sure it was one of the others.

He reckoned too, that just a pair of us was bad enough, but to get the three of us together was like three pairs, and as Jimmy said.

"Six little buggers."

Suddenly he would break into song.

"When I was a lad and had no sense." Totally out of character.

"I bought a fiddle for eighteen pence;
The only tune that I could play,
Was Mary get out of the donkey's way."

Much to our delight he would then substitute something else for fiddle and twist the other lines into a deal of naughtiness.

Another of his little ditties was half sung, and half said, a sort of chant. Here it is.

"There was a man and he went mad,
And he ran up a steeple,
And he cut off his tallywag,
And threw it at the people.

There was a lady passing by,
She thought it very funny;
She picked it up, and wiped it dry,
And sold it for some money."

The last line was often changed for something else; extremely rude, I might say, but then that was Jimmy, the little old man we all adored.

He was small in stature, wore britches and gaiters, tweed jacket and waistcoat, which sported a silver watch and chain; when dressed for market with collar and tie, or for a drive in his pony drawn tub he looked very smart indeed. He was never seen without wearing a cap; that is except once by Camp and myself; this particular day we went down to the woods, it was always down, never up, with Jimmy to fetch out a load of poles on the light timber trolley. Whilst loading up Camp picked up a long one on to his shoulder, swung it round and clouted Jimmy on the side of the head, dislodging his cap, and much to our surprise, exposing a bald and shining pate.

He looked so funny, we burst out laughing; this displeased Jimmy. He picked up his cap at the same time shouting.

"You little buggers. I'll break your bloody necks."

We scooted out of danger, and were too scared to rejoin him until he cooled down and assured us he would not hurt us, with the words.

"Come an you boys, I shan't 'urt ya, I knows 'twas only un accident."
On reflection it was obvious he wanted our assistance to get loaded up and back home in time for milking.

One day, Sam and I were almost fighting over who should use a certain little hay fork. Jimmy seeing this, said to me.

Jimmy off out for a ride; probably a summer's Sunday evening.

"You come with me Jack." He often called me Jack above water, or Jack under water. Why the reference to water, I never did hear.

There were all sorts of jacks, and lots of names like Jack Sprat; Jack and Jill; Jack-Frost, and Jack of all trades etc., but the reference to above and under-water is just as inexplicable today as it was then. It's not as though we bathed a lot in those days either. Only Jimmy knew what the inference was. Should have asked, but never did, so we'll never know.

On going to the shed he produced another smashing little fork, and gave it to me, with the words.

"This is your'n, so when you 'av done with it, put it back in 'ere, un you'll know we-er 'tis to morrer." Straight away committing me, although I was unaware of it at the time, to turn up and help again on the next day. At the same time, giving me the impression it was really mine.

Jimmy – thumb in waistcoat about to start his round

85

Chapter XX

A Whooping Time

One of the best and most outstanding times we ever had at school, or perhaps I should say, not at school when we should have been, was when there was an epidemic of whooping cough in the area. Although there were very few genuine cases in the school, I can remember that young Phil Harman; Nobby's and Brewer's little brother was one of them – he really was very ill.

We the pupils were told the best remedy for whooping cough was plenty of fresh air, which meant being out of doors as much as possible. Nobby and Brewer, although living in the same house as Phillip escaped catching the cough, so Nobby had the idea of pretending to Miss Goodenough the teacher that he had, and it worked.

He brought some pepper to school, and half way through Scripture lesson (first lesson of the day) sniffed some and sneezed three or four times, and with eyes streaming looked quite distressed. Teacher asked him.

"Have you been coughing George?"

"Yes Miss." Said George."

"And I whooped a few times last night."

"Oh dear." Said teacher.

"You had better go home, before you spread it round the rest of us." Then added. "Get as much fresh air as you can."

"Yes Miss. Thankyou Miss." Said Nobby, and off he went, grinning from ear to ear.

That was it, if Nob could do it so could the rest of us. In about a week most of we boys had pulled it off using the same technique as Nobby. What little liars we were, and how naughty it was to deceive teacher; but then with almost everybody doing it – it eleviated the guilt, and seemed to lessen the enormity of the wrong we had committed to such an extent, that in the end, there was no shame in any of us, and we were even congratulating ourselves on our achievement of being able to fill our lungs with lots of fresh air, and having a wonderful time, which in all lasted about six weeks.

Mr Nixey held a dozen ponies in a little field round the lane, that had never been ridden. His sons Ron, Bill and Len, were home with the so called whooping cough like the rest of us, and invited us to help with the breaking in of their dad's ponies.

All we had was a few halters, no saddles or bridles, but it was not long before we had broken them in, and were having bare-back rides every day. The stallions were the hardest to break in and the hardest to ride. In the end Mr Nixey insisted we gave them all a rest for a few days, or as he said. 'There would be nothing left of them.'

Never once did I hear a sneeze or a cough, and the only whoops were whoops' of joy and excitement as we galloped round and round the paddock like Indian braves and cowboys. The happiest and healthiest kids in all Bucks, Berks and Oxon.

Talking of riding, one of Moey's older brothers Reg had a Jack donkey, which it was said was impossible for nippers to ride; he used to buck and ass up, and tip them off wholesale. Moey was a good rider, and he had had him off a few times.

I reckoned I could ride a bit, after mastering those little stallions, so asked to have a go. My request granted, it was arranged for Saturday afternoon when Reg was home; news was put about, so there was quite a few gathered round when Jack was led out. Jock said. "He's been fed on beans all week in readiness for this." Which was no help to my nerves, as I began to wonder if I had bitten off more than I could chew. Still no backing out now, the halter end had been tied round the other side to form reins.

Somebody gave me a leg up, and away we went with Neddy pulling every stunt he knew. I let the halter drop on to his neck, and held on to his mane with both hands, and having fairly long legs gripped on to him like a leech. Round he swung, first one way and then the other. He reared up, he assed up, he did everything but give up, but I still stayed on and was just secretly congratulating myself when all of a sudden he sat down on his haunches like a dog, and off I slid on to my feet; there was nothing I could do about it but give him best. Everybody said they had never seen anything like it before, and congratulated me on my *stickability*. Donkeys were always said to be knowing and cunning, that one, certainly was.

Chapter XXI

Crabtree Barn

When I was about ten years old and Moey about twelve to thirteen his two brothers rented a sixteen acre field, with buildings adjoining of Mr Avery who owned Field Farm at the time, known as Crabtree Barn consisting of a large barn and other outbuildings, best described as laying in sheds for cattle. The buildings and field were approximately one and a half to two miles out of the village of Worminghall, and could be approached from about a mile up the Oakley Road, left down a grass lane known as Plumtree Lane on account there were some plumtrees a way down the lane that bore delicious white plums affording exquisite pleasure to we boys, the like I have never seen or tasted since. The lane

Ernest Joiner (Jock) As a young man.

ran thorough and alongside several large fields finally circumventing into Maul's Road – the Stanton St. John Road. This meant there was a choice of two ways to the field, where, during the summer months Reg, one of Moey's brothers kept a couple of cows, and Jock his other brother grazed his little bay stallion. The cows were used for calf rearing, which meant someone had to keep an eye on them, and often milk after a calf or calves had been taken away. It was mostly Moey's lot to do this after school with me going along to help, accompanied by the dogs; Moey with Jock's single barrelled twelve bore, and me with the white enamel pail. We used to hunt the hedgerows and bushes with the dogs for rabbits, and it was not often we came home with our pockets empty. It seems incredible on looking back, that boys so young as we were allowed to carry such a lethal weapon, but no one seemed to take any notice, except the local farmers whom we easily dodged, and if the copper was about we got off the highway, hiding ourselves and the gun until he had passed and out of sight. Besides which, if anyone had accosted us they would have had to answer to Jock who was no mean exponent if it came to fisticuffs.

Saturdays were great days for Moey and me, we would be up early, and off to the old barn, catch Joey the pony, often no simple task, harness and shut him into the two wheeled flat topped cart, load up and bring home a load ofleg wood to be sawn into blocks at a later date; then after dinner go back with Jock, probably with a load of hay or feed for the cows, hunting with the dogs, taking one way going, and the other coming back: It must be pointed out, that in those days and in the rural areas dinner-time was around midday, composed of meat and two veg., and lunch-time was mid-morning, usually consisting of a hunk of bread and cheese, and half an hour for lunch, but of course we boys were not strictly bound by times, and not having a watch gave us a good excuse if, and when we were late for meals.

Often we travelled home empty, and stood up on the little flat topped cart going 'Hell for Leather' down the Oakley Road, on down the Firs and straight over the crossroads at Townsend into the village, with Moey holding one rein and me the other to keep our balance, both shouting our heads off, and singing at the top of our voices –' Ahr Soldiers went to war, and Ahr Soldiers won, and Ahr Soldiers rammed their bayonets up the Kaiser's – Ah Soldiers' etc., a jolly roundelay methinks.

What with the singing, and the speed we were travelling accompanied by the rattling of the wheels and Joey's hooves on the flint road, all so exhilerating it seemed to act like a drug, making us both totally oblivious to any dangers that might befall us. Granted, there was but little traffic on the roads in those times, especially in the rural districts, but it did exist, and we were very fortunate not to meet anything on the crossroads, or I am sure, a terrible accident would have ensued, and Jock's friend – Fred Veary's (Dobbin's) words would have come true. He used to say.

'That bloody pony 'ull be the death of you boys.'

As before mentioned it was no easy task to catch 'that bloody pony' Dobbin called him, neither was it easy to harness him, talking of which, I learned the first piece of harness to put on a horse was the collar, but having been caught, one became wary when asked.

'Which part of the harness do you put on a horse first?'

There was so much back slang in those days, that if unwittingly one answered. 'The collar'. Then the quck retort would undoubtedly be.

'Collar my ass and lick it.'

To put the collar on Joey was no mean achievement, it took the two of us all our time and wiles, as he would invariably rear up, and strike out with his front hooves, rendering the whole operation pretty hazardous. This, of course, was after catching him. Often he would lead us a merry dance before we could slip the halter over his head.

One morning he gave us the round about so much we became so frustrated, almost to the point of tears, that after our second woodbine we decided to abandon the effort altogether, and go home. Then I said to Moey. 'What will Jock say?' Moey thought for a moment. Then replied.

'I know what 'e'll say. Fancy two bloody young wankers couldn't catch a pony.' When to our delight, and relief Joey came up to us and snuffled his nose into Moey's hand allowing him to halter him as nice as could be. Without doubt he had been having a game with us, and sensing we had given up became aware that we might go and leave him alone in that sixteen acre field for another week.

'You little bugger.' Moey exclaimed.

'I ought to give you a bloody good hiding.' At the same time patting and hugging his neck; knowing quite well he would do no such thing. How people could be unkind to such lovely creatures, I do not know.

Looking back well over half a century there often appears within the depths of ones mind, images without names; these figures swirl round and round like wraiths in a mist until they disappear then reappear, no clearer and still nameless; such is the case of the tall lean figure dressed in black, with a long white face, topped with a bowler hat. He could well pass as 'the man in black' except that instead of the executioners' axe, his hand holds a vicious looking bull-whip. Perhaps it is just as well that such as he should be lost, and remain nameless for ever.

Though never witnessing the alleged, dispicable cruelty of that particular tree haulier toward his team of horses, it was common knowledge those noble creatures would tremble at his shouted command, and that if he happened to be holding an iron-bar in his hand he would strike them with it, should his order not be obeyed; being but a child there was nothing I could do. After all these years the stories I heard still remain with me, and I wonder why no-one interfered, or reported him to the R.S.P.C.A. Thank goodness for the introduction of the steam engine which ousted the use of horses for timber hauling; ending the era of cruelty perpetrated by such as that figure in black, who perhaps, like the ghost in my mind is floating in space totally unacceptable to the keeper of those 'Pearly Gates.' Who knows?

Once when making our visit to the barn, a shot appeared imminent, Moe cocked the gun, but too late, before he got it to his shoulder the quarry vanished into the bushes leaving us with a cocked and loaded gun.

"Better fire it into the air." I suggested.

"What. And waste a cartridge?" Said he.

"Not bloody likely, we'll keep it cocked in case we see summut else to shoot at, and then uncock it when us gets there." That made sense. When we did get there, what a performance. He was afraid to pull the trigger and ease the hammer back with his thumb at the same time, like Jock did. In the end I held the hammer with both thumbs, and cased it down while he pulled the trigger; a good job it was a single and not a double with two triggers we might have pulled the wrong one.

I recall later in life when a similar incident occurred. I was out shooting with another of my pals – Cyril Wyatt (Squidge) who had a fourten, and asked to have a go with my twelve bore double. He too had cocked it.

"Better uncock it, and unload it." I said. "Before we crawl through the hedge." Adding. "Be sure and point it toward the ground." He did that all right, but pulled the wrong trigger corresponding to the hammer he was holding, and blasted the ground about a foot from my foot. Giving us both an unwelcome shock, and an experience not to be forgotten. But back to my story. On telling Jock what happened up at Crabtree he just laughed and said. "You little fools. You could have broken it and removed the cartridge, although it was cocked." I guess we looked a bit sheepish, but like everything else, it's easy when you know how.

One day, when going to Crabtree we went up Oakley Road, slipped through Little Masters, (the allotments) and across Barn Ground, One of Eddie Bury's fields, and 'lo and behold' Bill – Jock's dog grabbed an old hare in her form. Though Bill was reluctant to give it up Moey took it from him, and tried to break its neck by holding her, yes it was a doe, by the back legs and the back of the neck, the same as he did to break a rabbit's, but she was so long, and his arms were so outstretched he was unable to manage it.

'I'll 'old 'er legs, and you pull 'er 'ed.' I said. We tried this but to no avail.

'Buggered if I knows what to do. Said Moe.' I've sin Jock 'old a rabbut by the legs, and 'it it back of the 'ed with 's 'and un kill it. We'll try that.' So I held and Moey struck.

'Bugger that.' He said. That 'urt my bloody 'and, I could do it with a stooun.' Wonder the poor bloody thing hadn't died of fright by then. Anyway, we made our way to the stile, and found a suitable stone with which to bludgeon it and finally 'put it out of its misery.' as Moe's mum said, after hearing our story. That's not the end of it. Jock always said.

'If Bill catches a hare when he's with you boys, I'll give you half-a-crown.' Of course, he meant chase and catch it; what a thrill for us, just the thought of having so much doe. 'Doe gets dough' Said Moe.

'The witchy old hare'.

Bill was not quite good enough to run and catch a hare, but we spun Jock a tale, that we turned her up, and Bill cut across and turned her out of her track so when she got to the hedge she was out of her usual run, and so unable to get through, and that Bill caught her before she was able to make her getaway back into the field. Anyway we had the old hare to prove it, and Jock was so pleased, not that he wanted it, but that he could tell his mates of his dog's prowess. The fact Bill was a cunning hunter, and would often cut off a corner to catch a rabbit made our story more authentic. Moey and I got our halfcrown to buy a box of No. 3 cartridges for his little shotgun. Jock was happy, he usually bought our ammunition anyway, and as far as I know never knew but what Bill ran and caught the old hare, just as we two little sods had so aptly portrayed it. Though he did scare us a bit, he reckoned he had heard that some of the old witches turned themselves into a hare, and that some old lady had been found dead with the back of her head knocked in about the time we had killed the old hare. 'They reckon she was murdered. I shouldn't tell anybody if I was you.' It sure made the hairs prickle on the back of my neck, Moe said his did too, and we never ever breathed a word to anyone.

The old type haybarns were constructed with very high and wide double doors, to each side, and central so a loaded waggon could be drawn in from either side, and out the other after being unloaded; one particular year the hay was stacked up almost eaves high on both sides. Most likely old hay from a previous year, because that Spring we discovered a kestrel's nest in one corner on top of the hay, and a french owls' diagonally opposite on the other. The kestrel's had four eggs, and the owl's two. I took one of the kestrels for my collection, and of course boasted to Baggy Edwards of my find. At first I refused to tell him where the nest was, knowing full well he would go and take another egg for his collection. In the end he promised not to rob one if I told him its whereabouts, which like a fool I did, and as he said, we were good mates. The next visit confirmed my suspicions there were only two eggs in the nest, and though Baggy denied robbing it, I found out later that he had acquired a kestrels' from somewhere.

Both broods hatched out, two owls, two kestrels, all was well, but on the next visit a week later the two little owls were gone, and the little kestrels were dead in the nest, having been attacked by a bird or possibly a rat, but my theory even to this day was that the kestrel fed the owls to her young, and the mother owl killed the baby kestrels out of revenge. Just another of nature's mysteries never to be solved. At the same time bearing in mind the old saying. 'Nature in the raw is seldom mild.'

Chapter XXII

Spring and Summer Evenings

Most of the light evenings were taken up with either football or cricket. It was often said that the youth of Wornall started to play football when the season as such was over, undoubtedly this was a bit of an exaggeration: Townsend Ground was owned by Mr. Tanner of Upper Brook farm, and later by Mr. Kenneth Ware. 'Fast rider to the hounds,' as Dr. Baskin aptly depicted him, in the following poem. Besides which he was an enthusiastic cricketer and always a welcome member to the village team. The field referred to was always granted to the villagers as a sort of recreation ground, although we always called it the 'Cricket Ground.'

WORMINGHALL IN SPRINGTIME
by Dr Joseph Lougheed Baskin

In Worminghall when the plovers call,
And the brownflecked wren is seen,
When violets peep through their purple pall
From the banks of Thame so green.

Then folk that sit in inglenooks,
Each freezing winter night,
Come past the ivied oak and rooks,
Blue Chiltern Hills to sight.

Tis now the lichened thatch goes grey,
And stonecrop on red tile,
Turns succulent for coming May,
As spring scorns winter vile.

And down by Clifden Arms they say,
Where Fenn keeps all the fowl;
There Tom and Dick and all who may,
Drink good ale cheek by jowl.

The men pass at the blacksmith's door,
Where clang and clank are heard,
At seven in the morning hour,
With the sweet song of bird.

And when the old mare needs a nail,
In hoof, or mend in cart,
Stout George is there with fuels flare,
The forge hath willing heart.

Who is it rides that motor bike?
Just past the blacksmith's curve?
It is young Flintoff or his like,
He rides with careful verve.

Later upon their velvet green,
They play at Badminton,
The shuttles white fly fast and keen,
Through rays of setting sun.

So as we pass along the road,
The baker's cart goes by,
With goodies filled, brown and white bread,
And even loaves of rye.

While on the journey to Oxford,
The elms come into view,
Standing in silhouetted guard,
Against an azure blue.

Just now at Waterperry rock,
Gushes the limped stream,
And by the lane at Waterstock,
The drover drives his team.

On Sabbath, when the misty morn
Is rising o'er the dell,
What is that note sweet, yet forlorn,
That wafts across the fell.

Tis matins and our fathers here
Met in that chapel grey,
At festival and week and year,
As they oft do to day.

Go, quietly and gentle all,
You are on holy ground,
The vibrant bells of Worminghall,
Ring out their blissful sound.

Here comes on seventh day of calls,
When all the world is calm,
The one who in these sacred walls,
Seeks thoughts of holy balm.

And near is Hoddinott's farm, all prim,
As model as can be,
Neat stacks and hedges also trim;
The chimney smokes for tea.

Not far is Ware, of sporting fame,
Fast rider to the hounds,
And urchins who unlock his gate
Soon find they're out of bounds.

And as the evening draws along,
A van comes up the road,
Tis Hawes' bus from Worminghall,
From Ickford with its load.

When Worminghall in sun and shine,
The village lads will fill,
Then drawing near is Easter fine
Well known to Jack and Jill.

By courtesy of Mrs A. Dodwell

Many happy hours were spent kicking a football about, with jackets used as goalposts there would be practice of shooting in, and if enough turned up two teams would be formed; two captains, usually self appointed would toss up, and pick their players alternately. Whoever won the toss had the advantage, as naturally he always picked the best man first; still, that only made the so called weaker side all the more determined to beat them, adding zest to the game. One of the problems was the lack of a referee, all sorts of fouls were committed by both sides that it often developed into something more akin to rugby than football, especially considering the astronomical scores that often accrued.

Sometimes in the evenings Dad insisted I should help in the garden at one thing or another, but whatever it might be, as soon as I heard the sound of leather on willow I would want to be off, and to join in a knock about which had suddenly become the most important thing in life. I think Dad knew it, and would keep me hanging on until instead of helping being just a chore, it became an act of cruelty, or so it seemed to me. Then finally he would say.

'You can goo now boy.' No sooner had he said it than I was off like a long dog, 'hell for leather' down the garden paths, through the gate, down the road, through the stile, and into the cricket ground, happily taking in the situation, and adapting to it like a 'duck to water.'

It was an unwritten law that before you had a knock you were obliged to do a spell of fielding, which in affect, meant the chasing and retrieving that little sphere of leather, and throwing it back to the bowler, which obviously saved the chaps a lot of running about themselves.

Then, and when the older ones felt one had earned it one was granted a knock, and Froggy or George his brother, or who ever was bowling would toss up a few easy ones until they got fed up, and then look out, defend your wicket as best you could. I well remember once, after running around fielding all evening I had just got hold of the bat when I heard Mum shout.

'Vic, come on its gone eight.' That was the time I was supposed to be home. Being a nice evening she had walked down to the cricket stile. Fighting back the tears I dropped the bat, and ran off home hoping no one would see my great disappointment.

I suppose it was all those summers of practice, and my great enthusiasm for the game that contributed to my being 'not too bad at cricket,' especially as a bowler. We boys used to scratch up a team, and play a match or two against Ickford boys, also Shabbington, walking and carrying our gear with us across the fields when playing away. With our opponents doing the same when it was their turn to visit us.

At the age of twelve I was persuaded by Jock to play for the men's team. He was captain at the time, and payed my club subscription of one shilling and sixpence. When we played on a Saturday afternoon, which was not very often, the men's wives used to prepare a set tea for both teams charging a shilling a head, being the standard charge at the time; when playing at home I was able to pop home and so avoid having to pay my bob, and when playing away Jock came to the rescue again. Undoubtedly he thought me worth it, as with the aid of Jim Moore our umpire (Jock was captain always put me on the end he was umpiring) I invariably managed to take a good proportion of the wickets. Jim would say.

"Pitch it up about another six inches, you'll 'ave 'im.' Or sometimes "Bowl round the wicket and swing it across to 'is off, they'll catch 'im in the slips." If I kept to Jim's advice his tactics usually payed off. Sometimes a batsman inclined to stand across his wicket. Jim's advice would often be.

"Bowl over the wicket at 'is pads, but be sure and appeal if you 'its 'um I can't give 'im out or else." So on and so forth. Apparently he was an excellent wicket-keeper in his young days, and knew all the dodges. He was certainly a wiley old fox, and well worth the tuppence each of the team had to pay per match for his services as umpire. The only hat-trick to my credit was a controversial one. By taking the last two wickets consecutively in one match, and the first two in the next match with my first two balls. Making two hat-tricks, and yet, according to many no hat-trick at all. Still, four wickets with four balls, and the brief related glory that went with it was rewarding enough.

One of the few times we managed to beat Ickford ended in a culmination of excitement and tension. They needed two runs to win, with their last man, Walt Tipping to bat striding toward the wicket at the pavilion end, or rather where it would have been if we had had one, looking extremely cocky and oozing confidence. Woggy as he was called, was a short wirey little man, was right-handed, but at the same time Keck-handed. He grasped the handle of the bat with his left hand below that of his right and was reputed to be a tremendous hitter. As he took up position the Ickford supporters were shouting. "A six 'ull to Woggy – put 'er over the 'edge in ta middleground". Middleground being the next field to the cricket ground. I was bowling at the time, and had one more ball to complete the over. Jim our umpire took up his position at the wicket and asked Walt if he wanted centre.

"I dawnt want no bloody centre, sling a bugger up I'll sun show ee wether I wants centre or not." Jim must have been weighing up the situation, perhaps he didn't like Woggy much, or perhaps it was just his attitude he was at a difference with, anyway he turned to me and quietly said. "Give him a full toss straight at his bails." I'm sure to this day that is what he said. "Play." Shouts Jim all proper like. I takes my run looking as fierce and menacing as I could and let fly – so did Woggy, but being short he struck under the ball and-crash-his bails went flying. He slung his bat to the ground, I like to think more in disgust with himself than with me,

Ickford cricket team with supporters in the early 1920's.
Winners of The Long Crendon & District Cricket League
Perce Dover back row second right

though I did decide to keep a safe distance while he wore such a wild and demented look.

"Never in all my born days 'av I ever bin out to such a bloody ball as that – that ent crickut, bowling like that ought to be banned, along with the buggers what bowls such soddin' rubbish."

Then, as he made his way back to base he effused such a stream of invective the like never heard before or since on Wornall cricket ground. The stream becoming a torrent of foaming and frothing abuse cascading down a mountain side through a canyon of vituperation, ever fuming

James Moore (Jim) as a boy-chap.

and boiling with the B's just tiny bubbles compared to the other letters of alphabetical profanity.

I think the occasion was the better remembered by Walt's carrying on which, in spite of his futile protestations concluded in Wornall being triumphant over the old enemy, and at the same time affording a few of the seniors a legitimate excuse to get well and truly oiled; especially Jim who accepted full credit in conveying to me, just the mere perpetrator of his instructions, to deliver the full-tosser straight at his balls. Sorry bails. Good ol' Jim.

With the arrival of September and the ripening of the horse chestnuts, all male energies were directed toward collecting them in vast numbers. This meant the vigorous throwing of sticks up into the trees to dislodge them, followed by careful selection of what one considered to be the hardest and most suitable with which to play 'conkers'. Any surplus could be sold or swapped for lollies or fagcards.

Once obtained, came the process of boring a hole through the centre, a tedious job, usually with dad's old 'passer' or one of mum's meat skewers which more than often caused the 'conker' to split rendering it useless.

All sorts of tricks were used to try and produce a good 'hard-un' such as slightly roasting in the range oven; soaking in vinegar or laying out in the sun to harden off. I found that a leather washer from an old bicycle pump fitted between the bottom of the 'conker' and a large knot in the bottom of the string helped quite a bit. This was all right until the opposition found out, and kicked up saying it was unfair. Some even kept a 'last years' un.'

I think a 'tenner' was about the limit to which one lasted, though some claimed a 'fiftier' or more, but lots of fun was to be had with the almighty clash of self appointed champions, false declarations, and robust contradictions. Which on reflection would go something like this.

"I be champ, I got a 'sixer.'

"I know you ent, I got a 'sevener.'

"Liar."

"Cum on then, I'll sun show 'e." Then somebody would shout.

"I got a sixer, sell it for a 'a'penny." Hoping to trade with one of the girls. Who might respond with.

"I got 'a'penny but I've bin told to keep me 'and on it, I'll give'e four 'faggies' for it."

What ever the wit or banter all competitions were started with the rapid exclamation of.

"Obli, Obli O! My fust go!" Or possibly.

"Obli, Obli onk! My fust conk!

Who ever was judged to have gabbled it out quickest, had the privilege of first strike, which, if well placed would often result in a victory in one, and a conqueror at 'conkers'.

Perhaps one of the most pleasing and satisfying pastimes for the boys and chaps of the village was to stick up a row of bottles and jam-jars on the spinney hedge, and to throw and smash them.

There was always a good supply of ammunition in the form of flint stones that were used for road mending. These were conveniently placed in heaps, at intervals on the grass verges at the roadside, and were just a nice weight and size for throwing; there were always plenty of targets too, as the spinnies were used as dumping grounds by the cottagers who lived nearby. If we ran out of bottles and jars there was a plentiful supply of rusty tins to 'stick up'. I suppose 'stick up' came from the fact we stuck them up on specially prepared sticks. It was nice to hear the old tins rattle when we hit them, but no better feeling and sound than the crash of a smashed jam-jar or bottle from one's own efforts of combined accuracy and power.

If, as sometimes happened, one of the older villagers mildly remonstrated with something like.

"You bo-is 'ull cop it, throwing all them stoo-uns in that there spinney. There wunt be any left for roo-ud mending." The answer would likely be a good humoured repartee, such as.

Ready for target practice

"Us be practicing fer the fe-ast."

One of the best throwers, apart from 'Pan' (Walt Cross) was Froggy, he could throw and knock a 'gnats eye out' as it were, and at feast time the ladies of the village would give him their tanner and induce him to throw and win a coconut for them. It was four balls for a tanner, and not often Froggy failed to dislodge one with four balls. Often, weather permitting, he would be stripped out and sweating through his motivation and excitement, which seemed to impart itself to the onlookers, who would give out a cheer every time he won a coconut. That was, until in the end the stall-holder called a halt, as he growled the words.

"That 'ull do for tonight."

It was said, that the fair folks used to pay him to move on or not to throw at their coconut and 'touch'em' stalls. I have heard the same thing said of dart throwers' too. I do know that some of the best throwers have been banned at the local fairs by being quietly asked to move on.

Apart from an acquired skill at throwing, every young lad of nine or ten possessed a catapult, and with plenty of practice became quite accomplished with it. Some of the older boys used to go 'bird hocking' this was the dastardly act of shooting at a bird whilst it sat on its nest. Must admit to doing it once, fortunately I missed, and felt so disgusted with myself, that I refrained from ever doing it again, and did my best to influence others to my way of thinking.

I can remember having a home made sling, but was never able to obtain any accuracy with it; unlike David of biblical fame, who was obviously the object of my mimicry.

One of the best missiles for the catapult was a good heavy 'stoney' – A stone marble-so smooth and round it lent to great accuracy, and was conserved for shooting at worthwhile targets such as rabbits and pheasants.

Talking of marbles, this was a game much played in my young days. It was great if we boys could get a game of 'big-ring' with the chaps. This was played with two chalk marked rings, the centre one was about a foot across which held the marbles to be played for; each player subscribing the same amount, say anything from one to four. This centre ring was circumvented by a larger ring, also marked out with chalk, and about six feet in diameter. We would then lob up to decide the order of play. The one nearest to the centre ring going first and so on. I recollect it was better not to go too early as the first players were likely to move the object marbles out of the centre ring, and near to the edge of the outer ring making it easier for those who followed to knock them out of the big ring and so claim them; all shots were taken from the edge of the outside ring. If ones 'tawl' finished up in the big ring it became vulnerable, and if shot at and struck by another player was dead and out of the game, and any marbles he had won were handed over, sometimes a bit reluctantly, and often in short measure.

There were many variations to the rules, players could 'bag' first go, or 'lags last' or next to last or 'bag' second go, and so on. If a player's tawl rested in the centre ring it became dead and out of the game unless it had knocked out the last marble, so with the ring being empty the game would be over.

There was a lot of fun to be had when playing ordinary marbles, especially with blokes like Baggy and Tater taking part, if Baggy's tawl was under threat he would holler out.

"Knuckle down".

Then drop a bit of stick, and probably spit a big puddle between the tawls and shout.

"No move Tackle".

Anything to put you off. The only way to beat them was to shout out first.

"Knuckle up. Move tackle. No spetting." In anticipation of what they might do.

Woe betide if you moved the hand forward when shooting, they would shout.

"Dawnt count you fuggated."

To 'fuggat' was really a crime, and if you shot from off the thumb nail instead of the knuckle, they would laugh and say.

"Ah! Ah! Look at ol' 'cunny thumb.' He shoots like a gal. Give him abit of ribbon." Though such a method was a bit more accurate at short distances it was not worth the derisory remarks one would have to suffer. Get Taggy and his big hands up by the ring, he would 'fuggat' to such an extent he could sweep most of the marbles out of the ring with one shot leaving everybody to grab what they could. No good to argue with him, he was bigger than us.

There were several types of the marble itself. Very few were actually made of marble, the top grade was the 'alley' reserved for shooting with, called a tawl or taw, these were usually of pretty glass, a nice 'stoney' or a glass ginger procured from a ginger-beer, or lemonade bottle; next came the clays made from rolled clay and then baked, and finally the 'chalky' made from chalk and painted, these could be purchased at a low rate, about twelve a penny.

Most marble players had a favourite tawl with special markings, sometimes a clouded ginger we called a 'milky' – considered to be very lucky, and held to have superstitious means of power, when such powers decreased commensurate with ones skill, it was simply swapped for a different one.

Chapter XXIII

More Fun At Jimmy's

Whenever Jimmy had a good attendance of we boys, and some of the older chaps, which was very often, there was plenty of good natured banter and leg pulling. If someone was approaching with a view to join us, Jimmy would say 'let's catch o'l Sam, 'or who ever it might be.' Ask him if he can run. When he says yes. Say run your nose up my ass. 'Another one was.' Can you smell?' When the answer came back yes; who ever asked would say like lightning. 'Smell my ass.' Then there would be screams of laughter, and probably a bit of chasing by the victim.

If somebody was 'showing off a bit', bragging or swanking. The question would be put to him. "Do you fancy yourself?" Or possibly. "Fancy yourself dawnt you." Whatever the answer. "Yes." No, or not really." The quick retort was. "Stick a feather up yur ass un fancy you be a peacock then."

Should a hawk be hovering above, one dare not say. "Look there's a hawk." Or he would be quickly told. "Up his ass you walk." If somebody asked, "Can you punch?" And you thought you were clever and say. "No." Then you would be told. "Shit in your 'and and practice punching it then."

We were always trying to catch one another, so in a way I suppose it taught us to be smart, and always on the alert to avoid being made the butt of somebody's jokes, and become the laughing stock of the rest of the gang.

In spite of that I remember being caught twice in one day by Waggle. (Jack Sparks) He produced a John Player packet with the picture of the sea and a lighthouse on it, and asked. "Can you see the swan on there?" On studying it. I said "No, there 'ent one on there." He replied. "Yes there is." "Where is it then?" Says I, all innocent like. That was it. I had slipped up.

"Gone behind the lighthouse for a shit." Said Waggle with a grin of triumph. It was not often I was so easily caught; but like a rugby player, no matter how good you were, you were soon brought down to earth.

"That's a Good un." Was my response, with the thought of catching the next one who came along.

"Do you agree." said Waggle. "You must sell to buy again?" Certainly says I.

"Then sell your balls and buy some brains." Was the quick reply.

We had to make our own fun by trying to make fun of one or other of the present company. Often riddles were used such as. "When's a door not a door?" Everybody knew that one so you were pretty sure to catch someone. The secret was to say it quick and so prompt a quick answer. "When it's a jar." That was it. "Right, pee in it and drink my health." Was the quick reply.

One naughty little riddle that stands out in my memory is the one.

"Why's a monkey like a mole?" I used to tell my kids to ask their teachers that one, but nobody ever came up with the answer. I suppose they were not such dirty little devils as we were way back in the twenties. I never did disclose it to them, or to my grandchildren, so perhaps this is a good chance to do so. Here it is.

"Why's a monkey like a mole?"

"Because his tail's above his hole."

There was always a great deal of 'horse play' over at Jimmy's. When, and if somebody joined up with the gang with his hands in his pockets. One of the older ones present was likely to greet him with something such as.

"Wut Oh." Followed by his name or nick name.

"Pulled your puddin' lately?"

"Course not." Then somebody would be pretty sure to say.

"I'll bet 'es got 'oles in 'is pockuts. Let's 'av a look." Where upon he was grabbed, and his trouser pockets turned out. If he had big holes in them it was met with a cheer and laughter, followed by. "'E's joined the club, let's christen im." Where upon he would be floored, and his cock pulled out and spat upon. Often with the spit being rubbed in. If he had grown a few hairs then there would be another cheer and a shout.

"Ah! Look 'e's got some 'airs, Give 'im another dose somebody." There was nothing the victim could do about it, apart from struggle and swear. The odds were much too great, and there were very few, who, on reaching puberty escaped the ritual of being sworn in as a 'wanker'. Often referred to besides as 'pudding pulling;' 'bashing your bishop;' 'flogging your mutton', or 'wire pulling'.

There never was a dull moment when we all got together at Jimmy's to give him a helping hand.

Folks' used to say that Jimmy Kirtland was much too artful to die, but of course, that was not so; though, he did live to a good old age, and was greatly missed by all who knew him.

Chapter XXIV

Winter Evening Pastimes

It might be thought that living out in the country, back in the 1920's with no cinema, youth club, or any other public means of entertainment, there would be nothing for the lads of the village to do for recreation during the dark winter evenings. No such thing, providing the weather was kind they would congregate at one of the usual meeting points, often prearranged, and decide what to do from there.

If the weather was inclement we could always find shelter in Jimmy Kirtland's shed, and give him a hand chaff-cutting, wurzel grinding, or what ever. If it was fine and not too wet underfoot, it would probably be Fox and Hounds; two of the best runners would be selected as the fox, this meant they would have to keep together, have a minute or two start, and the rest of the gang (the hounds) give chase. The only clue as to direction the fox had taken was by voice, and the fact we all knew every gate, stile, gap or bridge in the locality, it was not too difficult to work out the trail taken. If foxed, one of the hounds would shout out. 'Oller. With the fox answering. "'Ere," or "'Over 'ere." Then off we would go again in hot pursuit, sweating and puffing.

Rarely was the fox caught, even if one half was captured the other usually managed to safely reach his den, which was the starting point. When we had all done the circuit, and everybody accounted for, there were many tales to relate; how ol' Nobby had "fell ass over head", and somebody else got stuck between the rails, or fallen into a ditch, or something else that caused a good laugh.

Many moonlight evenings were spent out in the cricket field trying to play football. We would split up into two teams, as equal as possible, with two little 'uns worth one big 'un. It was not so daft as it might appear, if a good dribbler got the ball he could take it unseen, right through and score. We must have had eyes like cats, though frequently someone would shout.

"Wheer is she?" She, meaning the ball – then the reply came back.

"Over 'ere." Then.

"Right, bung 'er athurt." And so on. The result being we kept warm chasing around until getting fed up, or the time came to pack up, and go home. Absolutely whacked out.

The Almshouses at Worminghall.

One of the favourite winter pastimes that created quite a deal of fun, was the celebrated 'window tapping'. I doubt if there is an elderly country gentleman living, who has not experienced it in one form or another; for the uninitiated I will try and explain how it worked. Materials required; one reel of thread, a safety pin, and a trouser button, attach the button to a short piece of thread, then tie the other end to the safety pin, so that when the pin is opened up and stuck into the window putty the button hangs down about six inches, leaving it free to tap the pane below. The next thing is to tie the end of the thread to just above the button, reel it out to a suitable hiding place, and gently give it a little pull and release it so the botton taps on the glass.

Often there would be no response from those within. I remember Dad used to say.

"Keep on my boys, You'll get fed up before I do."

Alternately, there were those who would quietly creep out and try to catch the culprits. I never heard of anyone being caught, but to be chased added to the excitement and made it all worth while. I must add that when and if someone came round to the window to investigate the tapping, whoever was working the contrivance gave it a little tug, pulling out the pin so the person could see nothing, possibly wondering what the cause might be, bearing in mind the old people were very conscious of ghosts, and an unexplained tapping could be quite eerie.

A story I feel must be related, although not being a witness to it I am sure of its credence through the fact of it being so often repeated by those who were.

Fairly late one evening, a little gang of the village youths decided to go window tapping round the almshouses. They set up on old Martha's window, and after a few minutes round came Recky Chadbone accompanied by Martha, and holding a lighted candle. Apparently the cotton being used was not very strong or got caught up, consequently breaking and leaving the pin and button in place. On seeing this Recky explained in detail to Martha just how he thought it worked in words more or less like this.

The early steam engine used for threshing and pulled by a pair of horses. Mr Veary the operator, was a Worminghall man.

"Well; well; well, what things they do act. 'eres the bloody ingin un' this is 'ow they fixes it. Dee see?

"Ah I siz." Says Martha. Then Recky continued. "They sticks this pin in 'ere like so; the button 'angs down 'ere, then they pulls this bit of cotton un' it guz – tippety tap – tippety tap." By this time the lads hiding behind the gooseberry bushes were almost wetting themselves laughing at the way Recky compared the technicalities of such a simple contrivance to that of an engine. The steam and combustion engine being the capital piece of industrial machinery of the period.

One wonders what the old dears of those days would have thought if they could have lived to see all the scientific developments of present day life. Although, I recall often saying with irrefutable conviction, long before the landing on the moon.

"They'll never put a man on the moon, as long as they have a hole up their backsides." How wrong I was. Now I say.

"If they can do that they can do anything." Just as I dare to say would those of Recky's era.

Sometimes during the late autumn, Froggy Hawes and Shoddy Joiner, who were great pals, would arrange an evening of sparrow dabbing, and much to our delight invite some of we young ones along to carry the quarry after extricating it from the net.

The equipment used was quite simple, comprising a piece of strawberry netting stretched between two bean rods about six feet long, placed roughly five feet apart, and cramped over and joined at the top, making sure a sack was formed by folding part of the netting back at the bottom to prevent any of the trapped birds escaping.

The chap with the net would walk on one side of a high hedge, and keep it outstretched by holding the bottom of the rods, ensuring it was held the right distance from the hedge, while someone else would walk slowly along on the other side bashing the hedge with another bean pole to drive out the roosting birds into the waiting net. As soon as the holder felt them hit it he would clap the poles together, and bring them down to the ground, at the same time shouting. "Whoa" to the basher, that was when we young ones came into action, shining the torch to see what birds were caught, take them out, appropriately dealing with them by either letting them go or killing them by just biting their heads, depending what they were. Then the 'holder upper' would shout. "Right" and off we would go again repeating the whole procedure.

Although the operation was referred to as 'sparrow dabbing' it was ever hoped a pheasant or two, and a few pigeons would be included in the catch.

With a gang of chaps and boys around, there was always a bit of sky-larking going on. On one occasion I well recall somebody on the bashing side shouting.

"Look out! There's a pheasant about! Sure enough something came hurtling into the net, almost taking it over Shoddy's head. He quickly

Reg Joiner (Shoddy) About to take off.

brought it to the ground, at the same time fearful it might escape shouting.

"Grab it boy." I grabbed it right enough; a bloody great wurzel. Of course, there were a few unprintable expletives flying around on our side of the hedge, and quite an amount of tittering and laughing on the other, but that particular incident was never forgotten, and always became the topic of conversation everytime the sparrow dabbing season came around.

It is true how the memory plays' tricks upon us, but I feel pretty sure it was Herb Cross (Moko) who created the 'flying wurzel', possibly because he always seemed highly amused when ever the subject was broached, often by himself, besides which, he was continually on the act at something or other.

Another moonlight pastime was high jumping by some of the more athletic of us – we would set up a horizontal bar, usually a bean rod on a couple of uprights pushed into the ground of the grass verge, often making the pole more visible by twisting one or two so called white handkerchiefs along it: Believe it or not, a few of us had a go at boxing by moonlight, until Campy got a blackeye, and we became physically aware how 'bloody daft it was' was Camp said. Still it caused a bit of a laugh among our elders, who were heard to say.

"Wonder what the bloody 'ell they'll get up to next." They didn't know half. Some nights a little gang of us would get down to Froggy's place at Pond Farm where, in one of the buildings he, and his brother had an old dartboard hung up over the manger with a candle as the sole means of illumination; after Froggy had declared, there was 'no need to waste paraffin', and had blown out the hurricane lamp. Friday and Saturday nights were favourite for this, as some of the older ones who had been payed would go to the pub, or send a couple of we young ones to collect a quart of draught beer, in the bottle kept for that specific purpose. Of course, we always had a good swig on the way back, and then insisted we had a drink for going, so after a couple of journeys we were quite jolly little fellows. As the evening went on there were a few tall stories told, about something that was supposed to have happened at work the other day, anything for a bit of fun; I remember one night somebody suggested – fifty with the lights out. No sooner said that done. Widdy had the darts. Nobby blew the light out, and dashed back out of line of fire, somebody shouted. "Right, stand well back." Widdy let fly. "plonk" went the dart.

"Sounds close!" Sam exclaimed with a chuckle. The next thing we knew a load of loose hay was raining down on us from the loft, and somebody had got up in the manger doing his best to drown us with pee, all at the same time. The language was decidedly mellow to say the least.

Froggy lit the candle. We knew who it was up in the loft kicking down the hay. That blooming Shoddy. But we never really knew who did the peeing, as he had quickly jumped down and joined the rest of us. There was lots of speculation coupled with accusations, and denials I had my own idea as suddenly a certain person bumped into me in the dark just

Albert Hawes (Froggy) All prepared to go rabbiting.

before the candle was lit. Anyway, he was bound to deny it, and was a lot bigger than me.

"Bloody 'ell." Widdy shouted. "I got a blinkin' fifty." Whether he had slipped up and stuck it in unobserved I don't know, but if he had not, I guess he's the only one to have fairly got, a bulls eye with the lights out.

This was all very well; all these going ons were wonderful, but the time quickly passed, and suddenly someone would realize just what the time actually was. The prevailing situation being, it was dark and a few of our homes were the other end of the village, so understandably we young ones liked to wait until an older one who lived up 'our end' was ready to go. This meant I for one, was always being chastised for arriving home late.

One evening, my older companion had gone his way leaving me on my own to scoot the rest of the way home. There were no street lights but there were all sorts of bogey men, lurking in likely, and unlikely places chiefly in ones imaginations, but they were certainly there, making it pointless in hanging around – and boy could I run – like the veritable wind. Anyway about a hundred yards from our gate I met someone coming my way up the middle of the road, the shape looking very much like Dads'. I put on the brakes, and on slowing down asked.

"Is that you Dad?"

"I'll Dad 'ee. "He said, as he made a move in my direction. I quickly dodged past him, and was home, boots off, upstairs, undressed, (there were no pyjamas in those nights) in bed, and under the clothes before I

Clifden Arms, Worminghall.

112

heard the outside door close, marking his arrival. I held my breath listening; a few minutes passed, and there were no footsteps on the stairs. Once again I had come through another exciting evening safe and unscathed. Not even a telling off till the next day, by which time I would have plenty of excuses, as Mum used to say. "A plaster for every sore."

'Better say my prayers; have always had to say them night and morning, but just say them in my mind now, not even out loud, Mum says that's all right as long as I say them.

"Our Father who art in Heaven."

'No! Better say my own first; the one I made up. I like that – hope God does.'

'I thank thee O'Lord God for bringing me safe this day through all perils and dangers, and pray that You will always do the same unto my lifes' end. Through Jesus Christ our Lord. Amen. In the mornings I say; this day and night.

'Our Father, who art in Heaven, Hallowed by thy name. Sunday tomorrow.' I'll sort out my fag-cards in the morning – hope it's fine. 'Only need a couple of wild flowers for a full set.'

'Where was I?'

"Hallowed be thy name. Thy Kingdom come. Thy will be done on earth, as it is in Heaven. Give us this day our daily bread." – 'I'll get a penny for bringing home Fonges's charity loaf from Church. Might get twopence; can't spend it till Monday though.'

"Our daily bread, and forgive us our treaspasses as we forgive them that trespass against us."

'Haven't been too bad today. I did sneak extra bit of sugar in my tea when Mum wasn't looking. I'd forgive her if t'was the other way round.'

"Lead us not into temptation."

'No! I don't say that any more. God doesn't lead us into temptation. The devil does that. Am sure God must be a bit upset with everybody suggesting He would lead them into temptation, by them asking Him not to. So now I say. Lead me away from temptation, and deliver me from evil, for Thine is the Kingdom the Power and the Glory, for ever and ever. Amen.'

Hope Alice Betterton comes to Church in the morning; if not I'll see her at Sunday school. She's pretty – I like her – I like her very much. Z Z Z!

It must be said those childhood prayers, with bits added to suit current situations have stayed with me, and stood me in good stead all my life. I sincerely hope. Indeed, I know they always will. Often the Lord's Prayer was interspersed with invading thoughts, especially after an exciting day causing disruption of that inner self, and making concentration almost impossible – it was then that nature would take over with somnolence evaporating the bombardment of extraneous thoughts into nothingness, once again causing those evening prayers to be only partly said.

With Jack being an engine driver on the Great Western Railway, and me fast approaching school leaving it was little wonder my future was being discussed, and the suggestion that he could get me an apprenticeship on the railway. Of course, it was revealed, I'd have to go into lodgings at Didcot, and would have to start at the bottom and work my way up, like he did. First 'a grease boy' which I didn't much like the sound of, then a cleaner, advancing to a stoker, finally a driver, only on the old tank engines to start with, but eventually qualifying for a Castle or a Queen, and a passenger train, just like him. For one thing, I had no intention of leaving home; a point I emphasised in no uncertain tones, with.

"I ent gooin' to leave 'ome, and I dawnt want to be a ingin driver anyway and thats that." Then adding, to give further weight to my pronouncement.

"All I wants to be when I grows up is a boxer. That's all I've ever wanted to be."

"Lot of bloody good that'll do you." Jack retorted. "Get yur bloody 'ead knocked off, and more than likely finish up punch drunk begging on the street corners." "I know I shan't." I countered. "I'll be too good for that; I'll be the best ever." Then after pausing. "I'll be like greased lightning and pack a punch like a mule kicking. You'll see." "I'll see all right." Scoffed Jack. "If you be gooin' to be any good at that game you needs to start now, not wait till you grows up." I guessed what he was leading up to. I'd sparred with him before and finished up with a bloody nose. "I got to goo un finish that bit of 'oeing for Dad." I said, nipping smartly by him and out of the door.

The next time Jack came home he proudly presented me with a boxing text book by 'Gentleman Jim Driscoll' Illustrated with real photographs of every move in the book. Forgive the pun, a complete and comprehensive manual in the art of self-defence. The left lead followed with a right cross; left jab, right uppercut, left and right hooks when in close; how too parry, block, weave, duck and dodge; no matter what ever move made to always return the gloves to the defensive position, always guarding the chin at the same time using the elbows to protect that other vital spot – the solar plexus.

The blow that impressed me most was the 'rabbit punch' in four smart moves; to duck or parry your opponents' left lead at the same time take a quick step to the right, and as he came by you a half turn to the left, followed with a mighty right to the nape of his neck. There was also a passage on 'Shadow Boxing', emphatic upon the benefits of cultivating the fluency of movement and balance.

My response to this was practice, and more practice. Never mind Jim Driscoll I was Len Harvey, Jack Hood and Jimmy Wilde, all rolled into one compact body of power speed and fortitude. Watching me one day. Dad opined. "It's all very well you dancing about like that it'll be a different story when you get some other ugly gret bugger throwing leather at ya." It was not long before I experienced the full implication of what proved to be, those few prophetic words.

Tommy Franklin had recently moved into Field Farm with his folks, and had started up an athletic club at Ickford, currently known as the Ickford and District Athletic Club. A few of we lads from Wornall payed our hard found fees and joined those noble associates in an endeavour, coupled with a great deal of enthusiasm to develop a sound and healthy mind within a strong and healthy body. On my first visit to the clubhouse, and the initial exercises over. Tommy who had a body like Adonis, and was an ardent participant in the fight game (he had gone ten rounds with Sid Cherry the local pugilist) decided upon a little boxing session in the form of a friendly bout. "Right Vic." He said. "You and Perce are about the same weight. Put the gloves on him Stan." To Stan Brown. "He's heavier than me an' older too." I interjected. "No there's not much in it, you've got a longer reach than him." Then as though spurred on in the anticipation of what to him might be an amusing spectacle. "We'll do this properly, three two minute rounds, I'll be ref, and coach at the same time. Stan you be time keeper and Eric (Eric Slade) you and Jocky (Jack Cross from Shabbington) can be Vic's seconds." Any further protests by me were brusquely brushed aside or completely ignored. The next few minutes found me gloved up and seated on a hard backed chair, an unwilling participant in a situation, which at that moment there was nowhere where I wouldn't rather be. Looking across at Perce Dover in the opposite corner – I knew Perce well, but as he sat there glaring across at me I realised he had a neck like one of Ralph Hoddinot's shorthorn bullocks, was about four foot wide, and that I must be giving him at least a stone. Still I assured myself, it was only a friendly bout, not that Perce was any great friend of anybody from Wornall. Not to panic, keep your head, thats a thought, just bring the long practised Driscoll techniques into action.

"Seconds out – Time." Shouts Stan as he clouted the old buckled triangle with a chair leg. I stepped tenatatively into the space provided, not Perce, he came thundering over toward me with both arms flailing like a windmill. 'Bloody 'ell' I thinks, as I slipped out of his path. "Stick your left out and keep 'im at bay." Shouts Tom. "Some hopes, he was like a bloody hurricane, my only hope was to keep out of his way. "Keep moving to the left." Shouted Tom as he dodged out of my path. This I managed to do, and after what seemed about ten minutes, and as Stan shouted. "Time." I realised I hadn't faired too badly, my left ear tingled a bit, that apart I was still in one piece, my head intact, no thanks to Perce who I thought had done his utmost to disloge it. "You're doing all right." Said Eric as he flapped a sweaty towel in my face. "Keep sticking that left out, and keep your guard up." "Seconds out – Time." Shouted Stan as he struck the old triangle, giving the impression he revelled in summoning somebody to his doom. I moved out intent on using the same self-preservative tactics as in the previous round, but Perce had slowed down a bit, and was picking his punches a bit better, and was delivering them with more accuracy, this presented me with a chance to use my textbook art of defence. "Keep on moving round away from his left." Shouted Tom. "How about his right." I queried, as I dodged past him. "Duck that." That's what I thought he said, so I ducked, straight into a vicious right hook which instantly brought into being an incadecence of illuminations far excelling anything conjured up by Blackpool. I managed to grab Sir Percival round the waist and hold on for a few seconds. "Break." Shouts Tom. "Step back." This I did, only to be caught by another right hook which started off a medley of bells ringing in my ears, madly and merrily as though they were celebrating some great occasion. "Time." Shouted Stan. That must be it – the end of the round. I staggered over toward my corner thinking how well the Merry Bells at Wheatley where ol' Jack Berry ran his boxing club was named. Eric grabbed me, pivoted me round on to the chair, and splashed some cold water in my face. "You're doing well – keep sticking that leftout, and not forget the right." whos' right I thought, his or mine, not likely I'd forget his bugger with my enthusiasm for this boxing lark fast waning towards zero. Jocky said. "Last round coming up you need this one, he's tiring a bit." As though we were fighting for a bloody title or something. Perhaps that was it, the Ickford and Wornall championship. "Seconds out third and last round – Time." Shouted Stan. Jock and Eric lifted me off the chair and pushed me out to meet the oncoming Perce. Didn't look as though he was tiring much. "Stop." Screamed Tom. "Touch gloves and step back." I stepped back, but Perce quickly discerning an opportunity to get the advantage, stepped forward forcing me to take evasive action by clinching and getting a bit of respite from an ensuing onslaught. "Break." Ordered Tom. As Perce relaxed I caught him with a lovely left jab which only succeeded in raising his ire, resultant in his chasing me all the harder with a more vicious glare in his eyes forcing me to muster all my wits to dodge his relentless bombardment. Round and round we went, faster and faster, snorting and blowing, ducking and diving. Now was the time to introduce and execute 'Gentleman Jim's technique'. The 'coup de grace' in the form of the 'rabbit punch' that I had practised a thousand times. This was it. Suddenly as he slammed his foot and lunged out with his left, I ducked, took a quick step to my right and as I rose half turned to the left, and as he passed me let drive with a beautiful right-hander Driscoll would have been proud of, bang behind the ear. What with the force of the blow and the impetous of Perce's lunge he went hurtling headlong into the side of the ring which happened to be a stack of clubhouse chairs. Crash, Perce had somehow got over on to his back, and with his eyes wide open looked surprised and shocked staring up at the arc-lights which in this instance was a sixty watt bulb. I thought how comfortable he looked. "Time." Roared Stan as he rattled the old triagle louder than ever. Tommy slapped his face and helped him to his feet; called me over; positioned himself between us and held up each one of our hands simultaneously, declaring what a grand contest it had been, and that draw was a proper and fair verdict. Then as he removed my gloves confided in me that we would have another session next week. I weakly nodded accent, at the same time thinking. Not if I bloody well know anything about it.

Next week came, and I gave it a miss as I had somehow developed a badly sprained wrist. I never sparred with Perce again, I feel due as much to his design as mine, but used to have 'em on with one of my mates, Widdy or Camp with whom I had a mutual agreement to take it easy, allowing that if one did inadvertently slap a bit hard it was aptly softened with a quick apology, supported by precautionary measures, just in case of subtle retaliations.

Chapter XXV

Proposition And Potential

As time went on my education advanced in all subjects; there were five of us always at the top of the class; Minnie Boyles; Dorothy Moore; Ron Nixey; Ada Barrett and myself. It was always a toss up who would be first and who came second, as I remember, we all had our share of firsts.

The only subject I was weak on was music, a subject, I considered of little importance at the time, and consequently was always being kept in at dinner-time following a singing lesson; some of the other boys used to pull my leg, saying she only kept me in because she liked me, besides other things, best forgotten.

The two songs equally hated by me were – 'Cherry Ripe' and 'Caller Herrin', week after week Miss Goodenough kept me back and made me go through them as she struck out the notes on the piano, but what was gained one week was lost again by the next, until thankfully, she gave up in despair.

Another thing I could not get on with too well was dancing. Not that I was the only one. One morning, when it was too wet to go outside for drill. She suddenly (Miss Goddenough) took it into her head she would teach the older ones 'Folk Dancing' – 'Rufty Tufty', and 'Gathering Peasecods', etc. We big boys were set to move some of the desks out of the way, so as to make sufficient space for two rows of us, seven or eight boys lined up on one side, and opposite, on the either side an equal amount of girls. They loved it. Then she played the tune of 'Rufty Tufty' on the piano.

"So as to familiarise you with it." She said. After which we were given a demonstration of the steps, which we had to practice to her humming the tune. Really all it was in the first movement was to dance forward to meet the girls in the centre of the floor, and then back again; this was quite enjoyable, especially the meeting in the middle bit. Having mastered this to our teachers' satisfaction we had to practice it to the music. That was when the fun started. Seven or eight of us, all wearing hobnailed boots, suddenly realising the more we stamped on the wooden floor, the more noise we could make. What with this and the thumping of the piano – anyone outside must have wondered whatever was going on.

"Stop! Stop! Stop!" She shouted. "You're more like cart horses than dancers." Then added. "Right, all boots off, and up against the wall." This caused another ripple of mirth as we all sat on the floor removing our boots; exposing a few holes, and according to some, releasing a few cheesy smells.

It is amazing how, when we should not we can always find something not quite in keeping with the current situation to amuse us, and to laugh at. Possibly an Englishman's sense of humour stems from such moments experienced during his school days.

"Right you boys, let's try again." Then. "On your toes and the balls of your feet." Another titter as Sam said in a posh sort of whisper.

"Are you dancing on your balls – of your feet?"

'RUFTY TUFTY' DAYS, WORMINGHAM SCHOOL 1927
BACK ROW: Leonard Nixey, Ronald Boyles, Harold Carpenter, Prinney Barratt, Millice Hornett, Richard Hill, Rupert Betterton & Victor Boyles, Ronald Nixey & Victor Hawes.
SECOND ROW: Ada Barrat, Hilda Baldwin, Alma Packer & Mildred Hornett.
THIRD ROW: Frances Baldwin, Betty Packer, Minnie Boyles, Dorothy Moore, Doris Dover, Owen Dover & Cyril Wyatt.

FOURTH ROW: Gladys Brooks, ? Betterton, Gerald Nixey & Beryl Neal.
FIFTH ROW: Arthur Wyatt, Philip Harman, Aubrey Hornett, Basil Mills, Robert Brooks, ? Betterton, Freda Mott, Hilda Atwell, Amey Hawes & Marjorie Moore.
SIXTH ROW: Ernest Bowler, Arthur Brooks, Roy Woodford, Joan Mott, Linda Joiner, Basil Hornett, Jack Nixey, Eric Veary & John Baldein.
In the background is the Photographers Motor Cycle & Mrs Parsons Bull Nosed Morris.

Apparently the first lesson was satisfactory without our hobnails, and as somebody remarked afterwards when recalling the event.

"We wuz prancing about like a lot of bloomin' gret fairys."

Singing and dancing apart it was understood I was quite bright in all the other subjects, with composition and essays being my strong point; I well remember how my old desk mate used to wonder at my ability to write two or three pages, while he struggled on two or three lines. Anyway, at the age of eleven Miss Goodenough said I should sit an exam for a scholarship to Thame Grammar School.

My greatest aspiration was to leave school; go to work, and have a shilling in my pocket. Somehow, for a lad to get a job and be earning was really something, a cardinal point in his life; he was suddenly elevated from being just a kid into someone who could have an opinion, thrust his hands into his trouser pockets, and jingle a few coins, even though they were only coppers, besides, he could swank and swagger a bit, and go down to pub, and buy a packet of crisps or a bottle of fizzy lemonade, sometimes if funds would run to it, a packet of woodbines; (they would always serve a young one providing he said they were for one of the chaps,) all privileges enjoyed by a lot of my older mates.

So in spite of pressure from all quarters I refused point blank to even consider sitting an exam, much to my regret afterwards when having to cycle almost five miles each way, night and morning, leaving home about six thirty a.m., and getting home at the same time in the evening, after working in a sawmill all day, and wondering 'why was I born,' and asking myself, 'have I got this for the rest of my life?' As mother used to say. 'What fools we mortals are.'

I had a shilling in my pocket all right, that was all I did have, my wages were ten shillings a week and Mum needed nine of them for my keep, leaving me with just a bob, 5p in today's money after working (more like slaving) for forty eight hours.

Occasionally, as a special treat, and sacrificing all else we would bike to Thame to the pictures on a Saturday night. With just a shilling pocket money which was apportioned out as follows. Twopence to store bike; eightpence to go into cinema. This left twopence for chips from the fish and chip shop. Never did afford a piece of fish. Then bike the five miles home, completely broke until the next Friday.

Still the thought of another three years at school was bad enough, but to go on beyond that would be pure lunacy, or so I thought, the most ironical thing about it being that as the time drew nearer to leave school, the more I grew to like it, and regretted not taking the advice of my elders, so consoled myself with the thought, that I might not have passed anyway; how disappointing and humiliating that would have been.

Nobody at the age of eleven, had ever sat for a scholarship at Wornall, much more pass, so no reason to think why I should have been an exception.

Whatever we were not taught we were certainly taught our manners, and how to behave, with the emphasis on the maxim, "Manners maketh Man." Though on reflection I feel it has to be knowledge that takes that honour. With education and experience the father and mother of knowledge one must be knowledgeable to know ones manners. Hence the following rhyme.

Knowledge

Education; be it from experience, school or college;
Gives us a wealth of invaluable knowledge
But, the one thing it teaches without any doubt,
Is, for all that we know, we hardly know owt;
It helps us appreciate all things as they are,
From a small speck of dust, to a heavenly star;
It raises our standards, so our ways they improve;
Deepens our friendships, and strengthens our love.

To study all subjects, a formidable task;
What is the object? Quite well you might ask;
It gives us a wide, and clearer conception,
And helps to develop that sense of perception
So, whatever the problem or strange situation,
It is easily solved, by a swift calculation;
It helps us help others fully aware of their plight,
To avoid doing wrong, and to do what is right.

To read the best poetry, and books we can find,
Will allow us to peep in another man's mind;
To glean from such writings, much wisdom and wit,
And to learn from the words another has writ;
Without education, our mind's a blank page –
Our soul like an eagle, asleep in a cage;
So spread those wings outward, and grasp all you can;
And remember. It's 'Knowledge,' that "Maketh The Man."

V.H.

The End.

GLOSSARY

alluz – always
butty – a pal; chum; partner
athurt – across
spadger – sparrow
wurzel – mangold
fe-ast – feast
touch'ems – skittles
tanner – sixpence
carrying – carting hay or corn
rades – ropes attached to wooden uprights to hold the hayload from slipping
mawn't – must not
chaze – cheese
accull – act; work
never never – payment by instalments
wotchered – wet footed
scort – kick out boots or shoes
swade – swede
yorks – leather straps worn round the legs just below the knees
skeddadle – move off with celerity
ockered – awkward; upset; mildly irrate
lags last – claim to go last
bags fust goo – claim to go first
fuggat – to move the hand forward when shooting a marble
alley – the top grade of marble used as a tawl
ginger – a glass marble procured from a bottle
cunny thumb – a method of shooting a marble
milky – a clouded glass ginger
chalky – a marble made of chalk
tawl – a special marble used for shooting
taw – another term for tawl
clay – a marble rolled from clay, and baked
stoney – a grey stone marble
firing – fuel, wood and coal
stickability – doggedness, hanging on; especially applicable to one accomplished at darts
lollies – sweets
passer – gimlet
faggies – fagcards